Healthy, Ever After

Healthy, Ever After

Evergreen Principles for Vibrant Living

SANJIV S. CHAUDHARY

HAY HOUSE

HOUSE

HAY HOUSE INDIA

New Delhi • London • Sydney

Carlsbad, California • New York City

Hay House Publishers (India) Pvt. Ltd.
Muskaan Complex, Plot No.3, B-2 Vasant Kunj, New Delhi-110 070, India
Hay House Inc., PO Box 5100, Carlsbad, CA 92018-5100, USA
Hay House UK, Ltd., The Sixth Floor, Watson House, 54 Baker Street, W1U 7BU, UK
Hay House Australia Pty Ltd., 18/36 Ralph St., Alexandria NSW 2015, Australia

Email: contact@hayhouse.co.in
www.hayhouse.co.in

ISBN 978-81-19554-06-5
ISBN 978-81-19554-07-2 (ebook)

Printed at Repro India Limited

Dedicated to the Emissary of Health

The health of a family revolves around the woman of the house. Women often learn about health practices from their mothers, who, in turn, have learned from their ancestors. This lineage of wisdom creates a continuum of healthy living that transcends generations. It is their love, discipline, and care that make a family, community, and the planet a healthier and happier place. I believe women are Mother Nature's emissaries of health on the planet earth and I would like to dedicate this book to them.

Contents

Preface

It is a well-known fact that human health has deteriorated drastically over the years. Let's look at some indicating figures to grasp this better. By the end of this decade, 98 million Indians are feared to suffer from diabetes as per the international diabetes federation. By 2060, cancer deaths will double while the cases of dementia will triple. But the most astonishing fact is that today, the rate of death due to overconsumption is far more than people dying due to starvation, tobacco, and alcohol. And despite advancements and developments in the fields of technology and medicine, which have led to a significant improvement in the quality of life, the same factors have led to a degraded health quality. One of the reasons for it being that all this advancement has led to more availability and options when it comes to food items and that too at cheaper prices, resulting in a shoot up in calorie intake. As per a survey, the calorie intake was found to be more than 3,800 per person in US and China in 2017 as compared to 2,800 and 1,300 in 1960 respectively. In India as well, the calorie intake has increased to 2,600 per person as compared to 2,000 a few decades back. This, in turn, has led to an alarming eleven-fold increase in obesity amongst children and adolescents which has increased from 11 million in 1975 to 124 million in 2016.

Looking at the stats above is definitely alarming as it seems that we are living in unhealthier times and that it is only getting worse. But is it really so? As per the data available, the life expectancy across the world in 1800 was close to only 25 years. And we are referring to the times when diets were organic, there were no toxins in the air, and everyone had an active lifestyle because there were no machines and technology. While today, we consume imbalanced and chemically infested diets, live in a polluted environment, and technology has made our physical movements limited to just touch and press, yet the life expectancy in current times is 70 years. So, the question arises that if people in earlier times had a healthier lifestyle and better living conditions then why didn't they live longer? Though there are factors such as wars, medical inventions, natural disasters, etc. that contribute to the life expectancy of a period, we can see by this comparison that there is more to health than we usually consider. This book represents an endeavour to uncover those timeless principles of health that have proven effective across various civilisations and eras.

A couple of good lessons that the recent pandemic taught us are that your immunity is your responsibility and one can stay healthy, even when surroundings are unhealthy. In one of the surveys by PWC, 96 per cent of respondents agreed that the future of health care will be driven by individuals managing their health themselves by being preventive and disciplined in their daily lives. The pandemic also demonstrated that if human interventions are reduced, nature has the ability to heal itself within weeks. We noted that water in the rivers had cleaned itself during lockdowns and the air pollution level had dropped as well. Similarly, the human body has an amazing quality to heal itself if we simply follow evergreen health principles.

However, in the current era, though everyone has access to information on all kinds of subjects, including health, this abundance of information often presents contradictions that make it challenging to discern what to believe and what not to believe. In order to understand health in its totality, we will need to unlearn the practice of applying health knowledge in patches and instead learn the systematic way of sustaining holistic health. This book is all about exploring those underlying factors that contribute to holistic health and better living in a clear and concise manner. It covers all dimensions of health—psychological, physiological, spiritual, and social health—and shares the simple ways to understand and apply these health principles. All in all, this book will act as a complete, simple, and systematic guide on your journey to good health and a happy life!

My Quest for Health

My curiosity to understand health as a holistic art began in 1999 when my eight-month-old daughter suffered a severe stomach infection. She vomited and passed motions profusely throughout that dreadful night and as young parents, we could not do much as we did not know much. We kept praying until we managed to consult a doctor the next morning. Before we could explain her problem to the doctor, he merely touched her hand and prescribed a treatment. He casually drew a diagram on a newspaper to make us understand the seriousness of her health and gave us a prescription to follow for the next 24 hours. The remedy was simply to feed her more water than she throws out in any form, otherwise, the consequences would get worse. It was a simple prescription to follow, and we did what we were asked to do dutifully. The next day, when we visited him, he held her hand again and proclaimed that she was out of danger.

Life moved on, and we forgot about the incident. About twelve years later, I attended a forum where an experienced cardio surgeon was sharing heart care tips, and someone from the audience asked what tests one should regularly get done to monitor heart health. The doctor suggested TMC and ECG. However, after a pause, he also pointed out that there have been incidents where a person suffered a heart attack even when the reports from these tests showed no unhealthy stats. What he said after that took the audience by shock. He then told us that he too had suffered two heart attacks. After a pin-drop silence in the auditorium, someone commented, 'Should we only live by the grace of God then?' The doctor nodded and said, 'Science is definitely a helpful tool but there is certainly much more to health for us to understand.'

This episode reminded me of my daughter's incident, and I could see a strange similarity between the two. The cardiologist had inadvertently implied that the disease may reside in an organ, but the treatment may lie somewhere else. Today, the advancement of science in the field of health has led to bottomless rabbit holes and thereby, it has become hard to expect mastery from a specialist when it comes to the topic of overall health. Perhaps, there are easier ways to treat or read early indicators of a disease without being an expert. And I was able to relate to this aspect when the doctor was able to diagnose my daughter's problem by a gentle touch. I pondered about how a mere touch had the potential to reveal signs of disorders within the human body. This query made me further question whether it was possible to draw the secrets of health in a simple format that is easily comprehensible to the common person.

My inquisitiveness grew over the years and gradually turned into a passion to know more and more about ways to achieve wholesome health. For me, questions that seemed foolish and complex eventually became notable observations and remarkable insights. I started probing deeper into questions such as 'If junk food is bad for health, then how is it the staple diet of one of the healthiest countries in the world?', 'Does the height of a tree and size of a fruit indicate something?' and 'If health is a science, then how can a common person understand it?' Every question reinforced my belief that health cannot be as complicated as science has made it, and this led me in the direction of designing a plan for healthy living without the intellect and complexity of science.

This concept kept resonating in my mind and the curiosity of asking 'why' drove me to explore the core principles of health. This book is an attempt to understand, identify, and comprehend vital elements of health and how we can adapt them in today's fast-paced contemporary world.

Chapter I

Health: Myths and Facts

'Not knowing is true knowledge. Assuming to know is a disease.
First, realise that you are sick, and then you can move toward health.'

—Lao Tzu

The war between human knowledge and nature's intellect seems to never end. The exponential growth and advancement of the medical industry in the last two centuries has led to an increased mortality rate. This means we are living longer, but it certainly does not mean that we are living healthier. On the other hand, living the way our ancestors did is next to impossible now as our surroundings have completely transformed. The way we have altered our lifestyle, dietary habits, sleep patterns, etc. can't be undone easily. But even though our current lifestyle is a far cry from earlier times, healthy living is an evergreen concept and can be adjusted to any advancement, transformation, and time period. The only challenge is how one can adjust and adopt principles of healthy living.

Today, with a click of a button, we can access almost endless information regarding health and thus, it is no surprise that people know a lot more about health. We all know the importance of eating greens, living an active life, and reducing sugar, fat, salt, oil, etc. But is this information enough to achieve and sustain a healthy life? Also, do these practices work uniformly across all individuals? For example, we know that eating fruits is good for health, but do we know whether eating the same fruit every day works or whether this frequency differentiates with lifestyle habits, routine, and profession? We may not have questioned why bananas can be peeled/skinned more easily than apples and why is mother's milk more beneficial than cow's milk. And what do we mean by active living and are we designed to exercise? Without understanding health holistically and what forms its foundation, we cannot unlock its full potential. And only when we are able to peer through and separate myths from facts, can we live a more happy and fulfilling life.

Let us delve into a selection of pivotal myths and facts and determine their relevance within our contemporary health discourse.

Myths and Facts

It is widely believed that the modern-day lifestyle is one of the leading reasons for deteriorating health. If we are to believe that lifestyle changes are one of the core reasons for our failing health, then it implies that the current lifestyle diseases like cancer, diabetes, and heart diseases would not be present or prevalent during earlier times when everyone lived a more active life and in better living conditions. But the truth is that there is much evidence that proves the dominance of every type of lifestyle disease which is prevalent today during ancient and medieval times. Even the ten-thousand-year-old text, Vedas, makes mentions of diseased bodies and polluted environments. Investigation of mummies from 2000 BC has shown signs of death due to cancer. There is also evidence that shows that hundreds of deaths were caused due to diabetes, at a time when white sugar had not been yet invented. So, even though many sources might claim that the contemporary lifestyle is the sole reason for bad health in current times, the fact is that modern-day diseases and health challenges existed even when machines were not invented, only organic food was prevalent, and there were no toxins in the air. Such findings reinforce the fact that health is not a modern-day concern.

This fact also brings out a curious question how people are managing to live healthy today, when we have chemical-infused diets, the worst environment quality ever, and boundless unhealthy options all around us. So, if it's not the modern-day lifestyle, then what are other factors that might have contributed to this exponential rise in disease in earlier times? Many of us have experienced and believe that today's fast-paced and challenging life has led to more stress, which has become one of the major causes of health issues. By this logic, it would also mean that our ancestors never had any stress. But another school of thought also believes that life was more uncertain in earlier times, due to factors such as vulnerable territories, the terror of unlawfulness, constant fear of death, mass migration, cold-blooded wars and battles, the uncertainty of finding basic necessities, etc. Our grandparents were also worried about education, career, marriage, and money as we do today. We can even make the argument that human life is more empowered and peaceful today as compared to ancient times. Thus, to consider modern-day stress as a differentiator between a healthy and unhealthy lifestyle seems like a myth.

Another common cause that is stated for unhealthy life in current times is climate change. But again, if we research enough, we will find that this story too has no relevance when it comes to the matter of decline in overall health. Several studies show that climate change has been a common phenomenon. There are traces of an Egyptian kingdom collapse due to drought about 4,200 years ago. Some recent studies state that severe climate change forced Harappans to shift to safer places. All these findings reveal that the shift in climate has been a cyclic trend which has been the reason for the rise and fall of many civilisations and that this phenomenon is not exclusive to the world today.

Also, the term 'chemical' has been ingrained in our minds as a potentially hazardous element and this perception has arisen due to a lack of precise definition. In simple terms, a chemical can be understood as an extraction of certain properties. For example, consider the extraction of ghee from milk. Ghee, in this context, qualifies as a chemical. Similarly, the juice derived from fruit is another example of a chemical. This concept extends to medicinal salts and even to the polio injections that played a pivotal role in eradicating polio. It is worth noting that our bodies necessitate specific chemicals for optimal functioning. These chemicals are required within defined limits and in forms that facilitate the respective function. Contrary to common misconceptions, chemicals, when appropriately consumed, are not detrimental but rather contribute to our overall well-being. Our bodies themselves are an amalgamation of various chemicals that collaborate to facilitate physical actions and emotional responses.

It is also largely believed that air pollution is one of the main reasons for lung-related diseases and that it has been increasingly getting worse since the advent of the Industrial Revolution in the 1950s. And due to this unprecedented decline in air quality, nations worldwide were forced to form the air quality control policy. The US declared their first-ever policy in 1968 while India formed its own policy in 2014. However, as per the samples collected by the NOAA (National Oceanic and Atmospheric Agency) for the last three glacial cycles, the carbon level has been always around 200 ppm (particulate per million) level. It rose to the level of 400 marks only after 2002 and has been stagnant at the danger level mark ever since. Thus, this again shows that all the modern-day aspects that we consider as prime reasons for the degradation of health quality have always been there and the same applies to food and water quality.

So, we can see that the topic of health has always been besieged by myths, misconceptions, and controversial ideologies. And this is understandable as it not only concerns each one of us but is also one of the biggest industries as well. This, in turn, leads to further contradictions, disagreements, and misinformation, even among the prominent health advocates as there is so much at stake for different stakeholders in the industry.

An important point to realise here is that human lifestyle and habits have constantly been evolving and will continue to do so in the future as well. Thus, it is imperative for individuals to learn to master health for themselves and for that, one needs to know, first, what is health.

Chapter II

The Best Love

'If deeds done for others earn happiness, then unhealthy practices applied on the self, defy happiness too.'

Many of us have developed unhealthy habits out of ignorance or due to taking health casually. And in order to attain optimum health, we need to form a bond with ourselves. Simply put, when we show love and care for ourselves, good health follows. It is solely the absence of this principle that leads to unhealthy lifestyles and health issues.

Many a time, while crossing a temple on my way to the office, I would notice a long queue of beggars and poor people standing there for a meal. I also thought about the man who served food every day religiously. I always complimented his spirit and the effort he made to make this happen. He would have to plan everything in advance, buy vegetables, grocerioes, etc., get up very early in the morning to prepare the food, then load everything in order to bring it to the temple, and then distribute it, day after day with the same passion without expecting anything in return. I always admired his kindness and respect for humanity.

One day, I had to make a visit to the temple, and while going in, I noticed the same guy sitting on a bench in an adjacent park and smoking a cigarette to relieve himself. Well, to me, this whole incident revealed a fundamental aspect of life. And that aspect is not only the first rule of health but also the foundation of the entire philosophy of living a healthy and happy life. What he inadvertently conveyed was that feeding others meant that he didn't need to take care of himself. He had a healthy practice of feeding others, but an unhealthy habit of mistreating his own lungs. The truth is that when it comes to health, treating your own body and mind in the correct manner is of primary importance and there is no substitute for it.

If we contemplate this matter, we will realise that there are only two things in the entire universe which belong to a person, and those being his own body and mind. This bond is permanent, and we are the sole custodians of both. There is a quote that captures this perfectly:

> *'If kindness is one of the finest characteristics of human nature, practice it on yourself first.'*

The point to note here is that taking care of the self is not selfishness but rather a virtuous act. And in the above case, if there is an almighty power bestowing blessings on us on the basis of the good deeds we do for others, then will the same power not question the self-care and love you extend to your own body and mind? Where did the man get the strength and the courage to carry out the activity? What will hold his spirit day after day with the same passion and energy? Does this not count in our karma?

The truth is that treating oneself with the same benevolence and compassion that we advocate for others is the foremost principle for leading a meaningful and fulfilling life. And this requires honesty, respect, kindness, generosity, and discipline towards the self. In fact, there is no task more virtuous than taking care of the self and no task more sinful than neglecting our own well-being. It's crucial to recognise that the duality of good health and poor health is a choice within your control. You can either foster an environment conducive to ailments or nurture a reservoir of healing energies for optimal well-being. Ultimately, the power invariably rests with you.

But what does self-care imply? Self-care means taking care of your emotional, mental, and physical well-being. Meaning, it's all about understanding your body, mind, feelings, thoughts, behaviour, and actions, and building a strong bond with the body and the mind.

Remember that self-care and self-love are nutrients to the soul. It is the stepping stone on your journey towards good health and without it, good health can never be established. It is the foremost principle to adopt on your journey towards good health.

Chapter III

The Best Person

'We all are similar, but distinctively different.'

Approximately 75,000 years ago, the Tado volcano erupted in a super-explosion which led to conditions that left only a few thousand humans on the planet alive. Since mating pairs were reduced due to the extensive destruction, biologists consider that 99.5 per cent of the DNA in all humans is the same and it is only the remaining 0.5 per cent that differentiates us as individuals. Out of 84 million species known to humans, which is only one-fifth of the total that have ever existed, humans share 99 per cent of their DNA with chimpanzees, and it is just that 1 per cent (that amounts to 30 million genes), which distinguishes us as humans. As per an article titled 'What makes us different', it is alleged that these 30 million genes are in the cerebral cortex of the human brain—the part which assists us in thinking and imagining. Besides, the staggering fact is that the 0.5 per cent difference in DNA of human beings has made each one of us so unique that in the history of humankind, no two individuals are ever born alike.

This testimony can be extended further with the example of our internal mechanisms. Even though each one of our systems (respiratory system, excretory system, circulatory system, etc.) has a similar composition, every feature has a specific and individualistic behaviour and function. The liver accomplishes hundreds of functions and upholds the potential to regrow to its full size, even when it is reduced to one-fourth of its total size. The kidney filters blood more than a dozen times in an hour. In a lifespan, the skin renews about a thousand times. The human brain can amass information up to five *Britannia encyclopedias*. Likewise, every cell, tissue, and organ has its own vitality and endurance, even within two individuals with the same built height and diet.

Thus, what we consume, how much we exercise, our past ailments, heredity, genetics, as well as aspects such as our nativity, social status, climate and geography, and permutations and combinations of a thousand other factors provide us with our unique individuality.

In a test conducted by the Weizmann Institute of Science in Israel, a group of scientists carried out a study on a thousand individuals with varied backgrounds having no history of diabetes. They were fed tomatoes for several days to monitor their blood sugar level after each meal. The test proved that blood sugar levels varied in each individual and there were variations in the same person when the same test was conducted on a different day. And when their diets were personalised for each participant, the results showed an improvement in blood sugar levels. The study points out that universal diet recommendations are misleading, whereas customised diets designed according to our specific anatomy can help us stay healthy. Moreover, a similar diet plan can influence the sugar level of the same individual differently on a different day because each individual differs in his or her thoughts, behaviour, and daily routine patterns. These indicators also show the fact that health is an individualistic and daily approach instead of a universal one. Therefore, your description of health is unique to you and only you can achieve it.

Thus, the main take away is that the beauty of health is that it is not limited to any standard diet or compulsive exercise. And though there are largely accepted habits and approaches, ultimately, there are no strict rules that will apply to everybody. There is a significant number of people who have been living solely on a non-vegetarian diet. France has the greatest number of healthy people even though its staple diet is high in carbohydrates and sugar. Noodles, which is high in refined carbohydrate, is a staple diet of many Asian countries. The fact is that no one can find the personalised health recipe for you, other than you, yourself. Remember that you are unique, your journey is unique, your experiences are unique, and so is your health.

Chapter IV

The Best Treasure

'If there is anything above naturopathy, it is the mind.'

There is a treasure that has no physical presence, can't be seen or touched, and has no weight. These intrinsic features make this treasure the most elusive and complicated element of health. And this treasure is the mind.

The human mind has evolved to become an intricate and essential aspect of our lives and over the years, it has staged itself as the foundation of human civilisation. And when it comes to our health, our mind plays an equally crucial role not only in our psychological health but also physiological health. Even the best of diets, treatments, and health practices do not work with an unhealthy mind. Simply put, unless the psyche principles are aligned, health cannot be gained.

But the strange thing about studying a mind is that one needs to think with the same mind to visualise the mind and the same mind generates questions and finds answers to those questions and so on. Thus, the human mind is a mysterious entity but with the right approach, we can uncover all its secrets. In this section, we shall study the workings of the mind and its relationship with our physical health and also explore simple ways to optimise it.

Mental Health

With time, there has been a rapid increase in mind-related or psychological issues such as stress, anxiety, and depression. This, in turn, has led to an increase in demand for mind doctors and specialists such as psychologists, psychotherapists, etc. and life coaches who cater exclusively to mind health. However, if you observe closely, you will realise that an integral part of their process is that they lay out how one can study their own mind and thereby get a better understanding of its functioning and deeper workings. Because when it comes to treating a mind, the prescription primarily lies within the self.

In the following sections, we will look into how the human mind differs from the animal mind and why it is more prone to mental disorders.

Prime Reason for Mental Disorders

A question that might come up when discussing mental health is whether other creatures on the earth face similar issues as humans? Do they suffer from stress, anxiety, depression, and other mental issues as we do or are these issues exclusive to humankind?

We know that the human brain is very different from animal brains and when it comes to using brain energy to function, humans are far ahead of animals. Our closest animal relative, chimpanzees, uses 2 to 3 per cent of their total energy for their brain functioning while the human brain takes almost 25 per cent of the total body energy. Though there are some factors that contribute to this difference in brain energy, broadly speaking, chimpanzees too have a complex life cycle that involves developing life skills, procreating, communicating, coordinating, etc. They also have almost similar metabolic systems to ours. Then why is there such a vast difference in the brain energy distribution between the two species? Is this because we think more, feel more, and more importantly, stress and fear more? Let's look at this closely.

When a deer spots a lion, a chemical reaction kicks in and provides energy to the body to escape the lion. In medical language, this state caused by the chemical reaction is called stress or fear and it is necessary as it acts as a signal to the body to take necessary action to escape the threat. So, in a way, all animals face stress of some kind in their day-to-day life. Still, we don't find the prevalence of mental issues as we do in humans. One of the main reasons for this, as per psychologists, is that such reactions that induce stress and fear in animals are intermittent and thus, they do not affect their physical health significantly. But when these states become prolonged and occur repeatedly, it starts taking a toll on the body and makes it more prone to infections and diseases. And this is where humans differ from animals. We are able to sustain emotions and feelings of stress and fear which affect our mental as well as physical health. Such states are directly linked to the mind and because of the imaginative ability of humans, we can feel stress and fear even when the threat is not real. And if this happens on a regular basis, the brain requires more energy from the body in return. A deer does not imagine that a lion is going to attack it unless it sees a lion. But we humans can imagine grief, sorrow, happiness, anger, etc., even when a respective situation that might elicit such a feeling or emotion is not present.

Therefore, we can see that our ability to imagine and create unreal scenarios, especially negative ones, makes us victims of self-created stress which, in turn, leads to poor mental and physical health.

Principal Role of the Mind

As discussed before, even though the exact functioning of the mind might be a bit complicated to decipher, we know that one of its primary uses in our daily lives is thinking. We all know that feelings lead to emotions, emotions to actions, and actions produce experiences, and the same process is repeated moment after moment for every decision we make in our lives. And though most of us know this chain of events, what we may have not noted is that between every step, the mind has a choice to make. It has an option of what to see, what to think, and what to interpret, and based on these factors, it makes a choice. And that's the principal job of the mind—to make a choice. Thoughts will come anyway, but which thoughts are chosen, and which thoughts are rejected is the mind's prerogative. But with time, making choices and decisions—the principal job of a mind—

steadily becomes its behaviour or habit, and eventually its character. And if this character is built on negative habits, then it can start affecting our health.

When our eyes see some kind of sweets, our mind guides us on whether we should eat them or not. It makes this call by taking into account the facts stored in our brain. It registers, through imagination, all aspects related to this—the sweets' taste, the pleasure of eating them, whether they are healthy or not, etc. and then either decides to go ahead with the action or restrict it. But an interesting point to note here is that the mind has the power to overrule the facts shown by the brain data. In other words, the mind is the superior authority that can either choose to obey or disobey the brain and the brain has no control over the mind's decision. This way, if the mind keeps overruling the objective facts shown by the brain time after time, then it can result in unhealthy habits.

Therefore, having good coordination between the mind and the brain becomes of significant importance. This can be seen especially in the cases of unhealthy eating habits. Mostly, this happens because every time the body feels like eating something unhealthy or avoiding exercising, the mind overpowers the brain and loses control over the decision-making process.

In the ideal scenario, the brain with sufficient facts should dominate the mind, which is also required because the mind by nature tends to go by its feelings. The facts build up the confidence of the brain and make it more powerful in curtailing the feeling-based decisions of the mind. And having a powerful brain that doesn't get easily swayed by the mind indicates a healthy mind and body. On the other hand, if the brain is regularly being overpowered by the mind, then that is a sign of weak mental health. This constant battle between our feelings and facts plays throughout our daily lives. And the state of our mental health (how weak or strong it is) depends on how well we manage our facts and feelings battle. Invariably, it is challenging to monitor any scientific precepts of the mind in order to control feelings, since this process cannot be supervised by anyone else but you. Only the self can assess how powerful is the control of the brain, how well it employs facts, and how often it finds it appropriate to execute resolutions. If you have an inactive lifestyle or any other unhealthy signs, chances are either you are lacking knowledge of your health, or your feelings are mostly overpowering your facts.

The Art of Balancing Mind and Brain

From the above model, it might feel that the mind and feelings are antagonists but that's not the case. As stated before, even stress and fear are integral parts of our lives and have a specific role to play. In other words, negative thoughts are as important as positive thoughts. The reason why aircraft have exit doors is that somebody thought about a potential negative outcome at the time of designing the plane. It is a negative thought, but it helps to better prepare ourselves for any contingency situation.

So, we can see that we need a balanced dynamic of feelings and facts to optimise our mental health.

As for facts, they relate to our self-awareness and knowledge about our own health and well-being. This understanding is more structured and acquired through learning and consistent practise. On the other hand, feelings are capable of meandering in any direction, at various intensities, and at any given juncture. That's why the management of feelings takes on paramount significance, and this is where the crux of the battle for mental health lies. Hence, effectively controlling and guiding feelings becomes pivotal. And if we know where our feelings originate from and the stimulus that triggers them, we can preemptively wrest control of them at the root. Armed with this insight, we can better prepare ourselves and win the battle of mental health. Let's delve into this in greater detail.

A feeling is generated either by an external source or by imagining a situation or scenario. In short, in the first case, the stimulus comes from the outer world, while in the latter, it is self-generated by the mind. These two categories can be further subdivided into various events that trigger feelings. So, if we understand all these events that generate feelings, we can be more conscious of them and use them for our benefit. In the subsequent section, we shall understand various experiences responsible for generating a feeling and learn some principles to master them.

I. External Origin

'We cannot control the events of our life.
But we control our reaction to those events.'
—Mahatria Ra

The first thing to understand when trying to master your feelings is that feelings are a result of an experience and thus instead of grappling with feelings, we need to deal with the experience that enforces that particular feeling. So, in order to control our feelings, we need to understand the kind of event that we are facing, which is at the source of that feeling.

Many experiences we face in our lives are challenging, and it is the mind's job to decide how to deal with every event in a way that ensures optimum mental health. These experiences or situations are not under our control, and they do not come to us as per our whims and fancies. You may walk out of the house with a happy and positive mind frame, but somebody on the road may irritate you by honking unnecessarily. You may walk in for a meeting with a free mind to discuss, but something from other participants may spoil your mood. The world around us makes us more unhappy than happy. Such situations when happen consistently take us beyond the moderation limit and make us mentally unhealthy. Thus, it becomes highly important to learn to evaluate situations we face as only through this process can we control the feelings generated by these experiences.

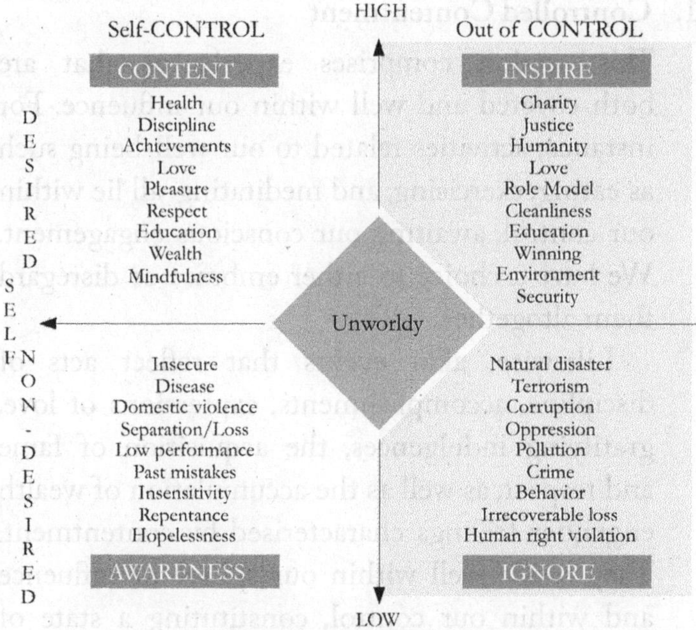

Mind Experience Zones

As shown in the 'Mind Experience Matrix', there are four types of experiences that arise in our day-to-day life, and they are either within our control or out of control. There are some experiences which we do ask for as shown in the 'Desired' section while there are some experiences which we do not want which have been marked as 'Non-Desired'. The matrix combines the various experiences into combinations of controlled versus desired and accommodates all situations of everyday routine and sets them into a list of feelings they generate. Now let's explore each category.

1. **Controlled Contentment**

   This section comprises experiences that are both coveted and well within our influence. For instance, activities related to our well-being such as eating, exercising, and meditating, all lie within our control, awaiting our conscious engagement. We have a choice to either embrace or disregard them altogether.

   Likewise, akin events that reflect acts of discipline, accomplishments, expressions of love, gratifying indulgences, the acquisition of fame and respect, as well as the accumulation of wealth engender feelings characterised by contentment. They reside well within our sphere of influence and within our control, constituting a state of happiness and the essence of wholesome living.

2. **Inspiring Experiences**

   These events mentioned in this section are beyond our control but still desirable. One feels great experiencing a new, beautiful city and situations that highlight equality, justice, humanity, love, good governance, respect, harmony, values, care for the environment, respect for human life and animals, empathy for the poor, etc. Such experiences inspire you and make you feel good.

3. **Conscious Awareness**

   Scenarios such as a relationship ending or someone getting ill are undesirable, but how to respond to these kinds of experiences is within our control. It's up to us to decide whether we continuously dwell on such experiences and allow them to persist in our minds or take action to manage them and move forward. For example, a disease can be treated by disciplined prescription, and a relationship can be saved by clarifying misunderstandings or accepting adjustments. Low performance on the job, unnecessary repentance of past blunders and worries about the future, are all controllable. We just need to be aware of such experiences and the kind of feelings they generate as it is the best way to tackle them.

4. **Selective Ignorance**

   Some of the challenging events are those which are never desired and also beyond our influence and control. Witnessing crime, miseries of the poor, inequality, racism, wars, riots, tyrants, oppression, bad governance, and exploitation generates negative feelings. For example, an ecologist will be perpetually unsettled about mounting plastic waste in the ocean. For experiences in this category, it is wise to be aware of how much that event takes up the mind. These are ideal events to go by facts over feelings and the earlier one learns to ignore them, the healthier it is.

   By understanding how these different categories of experiences generate feelings and exerting conscious control over our responses and reactions, we can enhance our emotional well-being and achieve a healthier and more balanced mindset.

In addition to the external experiences mentioned earlier, the mind has the capacity to envision or generate its own experiences, which are further elaborated upon below.

II. Internal Origin

'An uncontrolled mind will seek distractions.'

As discussed earlier, feelings are generated either by external events or by imaging events which may or may not be a reality. The feelings have the capacity to influence our moods and emotions and can broadly be confined to three levels:

- High
- Low
- Neutral

Here, high represents positive feelings such as happiness, low represents negative feelings such as sorrow and pessimism, and neutral denotes feelings such as peace and tranquillity. Likewise, we have only one state in which to contemplate life; we can either be in the present, preoccupied with the future, or dwelling on the past.

By plotting these permutations of high, low, and neutral levels with the past, present, and future states, the kind of feeling a mind generates are within the nine feeling spots as represented by the 'Mind Compass'.

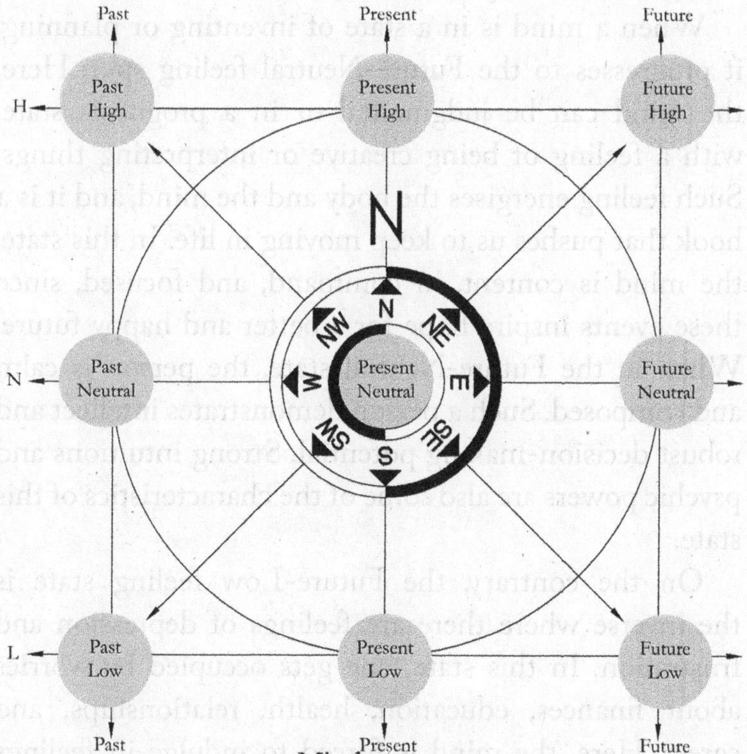

Mind compass

The above image depicts where a mind travels when it is in one of the nine states. When a mind wanders in the Future-High spot, it is in a happy state and experiences pleasure and optimism and generates feelings of hope, love, and success. Physiologically, such feelings do make the mind hyperactive which, in turn, keeps the blood circulation on the higher side. But if such feelings are momentary, they are healthy, and if prolonged they lead to disorders like high blood pressure and related diseases. Consistency, in this state, you can make a behavioural change and develop characteristics.

When a mind is in a state of inventing or planning, it progresses to the Future-Neutral feeling spot. Here, the mind can be judgmental or in a prognosis state, with a feeling of being creative or interpreting things. Such feeling energises the body and the mind, and it is a hook that pushes us to keep moving in life. In this state, the mind is content, in command, and focused, since these events inspire hope for a better and happy future. When in the Future-Neutral state, the person is calm and composed. Such a person demonstrates intellect and robust decision-making potential. Strong intuitions and psychic powers are also some of the characteristics of this state.

On the contrary, the Future-Low feeling state is the inverse where there are feelings of depression and frustration. In this state, one gets occupied by worries about finances, education, health, relationships, and career. Here, the mind is forced to indulge in feelings of adverse imagination and produces reactions of apprehension, jealousy, sadness, and hopelessness. A mind in this state is normally quiet and aloof. It is also one of the worst spots for overall health.

Moderately comparable to the latter, the Present-Low, denotes life's failures, tragedies, deaths, separations, financial crises, and inferiority complexes. Depending on the degree of loss, it leads to short-term stress or even long-term depression. However, the feelings of this state are temporary and do not last for long since they happen in the present and have the propensity to move to the memory (Past-Low). These situations necessitate robust emotional health and maturity since some of the most serious blunders like killing, suicide, theft, self-harm, and so on happen while the mind is in this spot. Like the above, it depletes the body's energy, weakens the digestive system, and enhances proximity to digestion-related diseases, boosting diabetes and asthma. Consequently, the Past-Low, which is the unhealthiest state for the mind, stores memories of tragedies, failures, and misfortunes. The feelings in this state comprise dullness, hopelessness, a lack of confidence, and apprehension. Consistently being in this state leads to weight or hair loss, early grey hair, pre-age wrinkles, frequent nervousness, restlessness, and lack of agility. Other characteristics of this state include a lack of enthusiasm and concentration, sporadic mood swings, pensiveness, a desire for self-harm, and feelings of guilt.

When a mind has to think about neutral events, which do not have much implication on moods or reactions, it is referred to as the Past-Neutral events. This state relates to calm feelings and requires the ability to be in the present while experiencing events. The Past-High state consists of retrieving feelings of happiness, fun, achievements, and joy and instilling and inspiring hope and positivity. When thinking about such feelings, the mind tends to remain hyperactive and energetic, but if this state is prolonged can, it can lead to hypertension-related disorders. Similar feelings occur when thinking about celebrations, winnings, or achievements that are happening in the present, denoted as the Present-High state.

Thus, our aim should be to control the mind and stay in the Present-Neutral state as it is a state of healthy feelings, healing, relaxation, tranquillity, and peace with oneself. It results in well-thought-out actions and emotions, which are not influenced by the highs and the lows of any situation. It is the place where the virtues of the soul wish to stay and attain knowledge, happiness, and wellness. So, we should train our mind to keep it returning to the Present-Neutral state, for wholesome mental health.

This Mind Compass is a mirror to the kinds of feeling a mind generates. All such feelings are self-controlled, and only a self-aware mind can restrict any feeling that goes beyond moderation, which is the key to optimum mental health.

FIT Principle: Control Your Feelings

'The healthiest and the unhealthiest moments for any human are when he or she is alone.'

People who have mastered the art of controlling their feelings often enjoy better mental and emotional well-being, which, in turn, contributes to a healthier and more balanced lifestyle. By now you know which event generates what feelings in you and where your mind wanders the most on the mind compass. But before we can attempt to control our feelings, we need to be able to identify our feelings in the first place. And by just controlling what to feel and how long to feel, we are able to take charge of our psychological health which, in turn, takes care of the majority of physiological health aspects. This is the reason why controlling our feelings is a prime principle of health. Now let's understand this principle in detail.

How are you feeling right now? Take a pause and answer this question. This would be the first step to building a healthy mind and body. According to American psychologist Robert Plutchik, there are eight broad types of feelings: fear, anger, sorrow, delight, shame, trust, hope, and surprise. To make it simple, they are either pleasant, unpleasant, or neutral, which is similar to the Mind Compass model representing High, Low, and Neutral states.

The beauty of the mind is that it does not lie and desires to spend time with itself. The best way to get closer to the mind is to be alone in a cosy quiet place with eyes closed. Focus on your breathing and then gradually, channelise your thoughts and recollect your day's proceedings. Recall all your experiences and reactions throughout the day.

Think about your family. Think about your friends one by one. What do you feel about them? Think about the people you do not like. What is it that you do not like about them? Think about the people you are jealous of and you have lied to. Do you love or miss someone? Are you happy and content with life? What worries you the most? What do you fear the most? What do people think of you? Did you do anything to make you happy and satisfied today? Think about all your body parts. Try to visualise your god, your idol, your favourite things, your love, and anything that makes you happy, or even sad. It could be a situation, a person, an incident, a relationship, etc.

With consistent assessment of your feelings, your mind will most certainly start to identify patterns of what feelings occupy it the most. It will gradually begin to learn to draw your attention to the present state of feelings. Note these patterns first and don't judge. With awareness, you will be able to enforce control.

If your objective is to be happy and content, then the realisation of sad and worrisome feelings can help turn them into pleasant feelings. Expressing yourself or writing your thoughts down can be healthy alternatives to liberating stress. Redoing your daily to-do list is the most practical way to adapt to the culture of self-satisfaction. It helps to divert stress and anxiety onto a piece of paper. Remember that unpleasant thoughts are like chemical-based processed diets, while pleasant ones are organic and nutritious. Positive body actions and words act as nutrients to the mind. Speaking motivational phrases like 'I will do it', 'I am good', 'All is well', 'It is temporary', 'I will manage it,' and 'I can still do it' helps the mind manage your feelings.

Conclusion

To summarise, our feelings shape the mind and body and are a cornerstone for a healthy life. And since every emotion has a physiological connection, it becomes crucial to control and know your feelings, keep them in moderation, and do not let them win over the facts. Another important point is that the relationship between the feelings and mind isn't one-sided; it operates bidirectionally. Meaning, even bodily cues communicate messages to the mind. This shows how the body can synergise with the mind, shaping a holistic connection. In the next chapter, we will see how the body complements the mind.

Chapter V

The Best Asset

'One of the best things we can do is look under the surface; we are all the same inside.'

—Randy Taran

We know that every individual is unique, but this doesn't imply that we all are completely different. A body may vary in its strength, endurance, agility, and shape, but all of us have two hands, two legs, a spine, and a pair of feet. Similarly, a face may differ in its features, but every face has two eyes, a nose, and a pair of lips. And we analyse this aspect closely, we will find that even though body frames come in various patterns and dimensions, the body parts never deviate from the assigned ratios and proportions as per mother nature's architecture. Even a tiny cell in a body has a defined ratio of size and energy in proportion to other parts like atoms, cells, tissues, muscle organs, and the body as a whole. But why are there universal ratios and proportions in the first place? Let's explore this in detail.

A group of atoms forms a cell, a cluster of cells makes a tissue, and layers of tissue develop an organ. Organs, along with muscles, bones, and the nervous system, construct a body. To hold the body together and balanced, the backbone holds the entire muscular and nervous system together and connects them to the brain. It is possible that the strength of a muscle may differ, but its size in proportion to surrounding muscles has to be within a specific ratio. Similarly, the efficacy of an organ may vary, but its size has to be in proportion to the body's height. The length of our veins and the number of muscles and bones in our body will always be proportionate to our weight and height. In the same manner, the internal composition of every muscle, nerve, and bone in the body is related to the amount of blood and flesh.

Such ratios and proportions in the human body don't end here. The length of the arms spread out wide is equal to body height. The length of the hand is one-tenth of body height and is equal to the length of the face, while the length of a foot is equal to the length of the forearm. The nose's length is equal to the first two portions of the index finger. Also, in all human bodies, water makes up for ninety-two per cent of the blood, three-fourths of the muscles and the brain, and two-thirds of the entire body. Even a minor disproportion in any of these ratios, from a cell to the entire body, can have a significant impact. These dimensions indicate the meticulous precision of nature, identifying a balance between muscle strength, body weight, and ratios for ideal physical health and workability.

And due to the meticulous balance and precise proportions dictated by Mother Nature, even the slightest deviation can disrupt the intricate harmony of bodily alignment. Such deviations result in misalignment, which serves as a clear indicator of an unhealthy physique. And by utilising these size ratios and proportions, we can gain the ability to make precise diagnoses of health-related aspects. This methodology is used in evaluating the well-being of internal organs through some physical tests. For our present discussion, we will delve into a selection of crucial physiological health parameters that hold the utmost significance for physical well-being.

Body Health Dimensions

- **BMI**

  Body Mass Index, commonly known as BMI, is a tool that can help us ascertain the amount of fat in the body. To calculate BMI, the factors that we need to take into account are gender, age, weight, and height. As per the American Heart Association, the ideal BMI range for men is 18.5 to 24.9 and 24 to 29.8 for women, though can vary by age.

  However, health experts do not consider BMI as a prominent health parameter, since it does indicate the ratio of fat, but it does not account for where the fat is located. Apart from knowing how much fat a body carries, it is more important to know where it carries. Also, a person can still be unhealthy with a healthy BMI if the fat is disproportionately distributed. To identify the position of the extra fat, a simple in-house test can be performed and it is as follows.

Align your ears in line with your shoulders and stand with your feet open, parallel to the shoulders. You can stand in front of a full-sized mirror, if available. Next, jump one to two inches above the ground. The thing to notice here is that while jumping, the parts of your body with extra fat will not be in sync with the rhythm of the jump, i.e., the fatty portions will not move with the jump but follow the jump. The parts with excess fat can be noticed in the mirror or felt with the eyes closed. This general test will help you spot where all fat has accumulated in your body. If you have more fat around the waist and stomach, this means your most crucial muscles are cramped and that they are affecting the respiratory and excretory systems overall functioning. On the other hand, if you have more fat around your thighs, hips, and arms, these are signs that you are not feeling active most part of the day. On the other hand, a naturally proportionate body should feel light during the jumping movement around the chest and the front abdominal portion.

- Waist

One of the clearest ways to know the health of a person is by noticing the outline of the waist. It is one of the primary statistics, indicating physical health and unless the waist or the midsection is within the ideal range, the body is bound to be unfit and unhealthy. But what is this ideal range for waist size? This can be calculated through the waist-to-height ratio. The muscles in the midsection, especially around the stomach and to the side of the waist, are the least used in daily life. The only time abdominal muscles are used is when a body gets up from the sleeping position without elbow support or when you sit and get up during squats. If a body is inadvertently used to taking elbow or hand support while getting up, these muscles start getting stagnant and become prone to accumulating fat, making the body visually disproportionate. In short, a disproportionate midsection is a sign of physical disorder.

Ideally, the waist size should be between 42 to 50 per cent of body height. If the body height is 68 inches (5 feet 8 inches), then a waist size between 29 to 35 inches is considered healthy. Any discrepancy in this ratio affects the upper body muscles by putting consistent strain on the spine and on the lower back to hold it upright. And if one is not conscious of their posture, the body eventually surrenders to a slouching posture which compresses the organs around the stomach, enhancing the risk of respiratory and digestion-related diseases. Anything above 50 per cent is generally considered overweight and 63 per cent or more is considered obese.

During the jumping test, bodies with more than a 50 per cent waist-to-height ratio will undoubtedly have more movement around the waist. Similarly, the hip-to-waist ratio should be around 80 per cent for males and 70 per cent for females as per the World Health Organisation. So, if the circumference of the hip is 100 cm, then the waist should be less than or between 85 to 90 cm in males and 75 to 80 cm in females. Anything between 85cm and 95cm is manageable, but beyond that, the body will become pear-shaped and prone to diseases. This can be also seen in the manner that the lesser the distance between the belly button and the spine, the easier it is for the spine to hold the body weight and keep it straight.

- **Shoulders**

People without a regular exercise routine may struggle to count the number of times in a day, they lift their hands above their head. That is because there are hardly any such instances in our routine life that require raising our hands above our head, and this is one of the prime reasons for frozen shoulders. Uneasiness in rotating the arms straight and full and holding them horizontally are some of the common symptoms of rotator cuff. While moving, the health of the shoulders is important for upper body fitness and strength.

Other than injury, the cause of any shoulder pain could be because of three fundamental reasons: improper alignment, weakness, or tight muscles. The cause for these issues could vary from poor posture to stagnation of shoulder muscles due to less use to sleeping on the shoulders. To determine shoulder alignment, keep a thumb on the collarbone and the first finger of the same hand on the cheekbone while standing in a natural posture. If they are not in a straight line, it is a sign of a non-aligned shoulder. Generally, in non-aligned postures, the head drops forward and puts a consistent load on the cervical and upper back muscles. The improper posture can magnify weight to six times the standard weight. If the weight of the head is 4 kilos, it will seem like 22 kilos.

A simple test that you conduct to know whether or not you have stiff shoulders is as follows. Place a hand on the lower back, parallel to the elbow, with your palm open outside. Now slowly turn the palm inwards by twisting the wrist. If the upper back shoulder spatula points out, it indicates a stiff shoulder. Another indicator is that while standing casually with fingers folded in and thumbs sticking out, your thumb will point towards your thighs in case of slouched shoulders and a well-aligned shoulder will keep it facing forward.

- Feet

If the backbone holds the whole body up, then it is the task of the feet to balance the entire body's weight. Any alignment which is not in line with the Earth's gravity leads to imbalance. This is a common issue but many people suffering from back, knee, hamstring, or hip pain, don't realise that the simple solution lies in the alignment of their feet. Our feet have been designed in a way that they not only bear the body load but also absorb and adjust to the shocks with the arch of feet. A collapsed arch on the floor while walking, running, or sitting could cause pain or assign an extra load to the muscles. This, in turn, can disrupt coordinating muscle strength and if prolonged, it can lead to joint pain.

A simple footprint can help us determine the health of joints, hamstring, calves, and shin muscles and the shape of the arch defines the health of the four major joints: ankle, knee, hip, and shoulders. Thus, a simple wet test can give us a good idea of the health and status of the overall body alignment. In order to conduct a wet test, you will need to wet your bare sole and take a print on a sheet of paper. Next, draw a rough line close to wet portions as illustrated in the diagram on next page.

Next, classify the shape of your feet as normal, high, or flat-foot based on the design drawn. A normal arch print will show more than half-arch coverage within the ankle and front toe as shown in the figure. In the normal shape, the feet are aligned and handle the body weight on the muscles which are designed to handle the weight as per nature's design. But the point to be noted here is that even with the normal arch, if the body posture is not in line with the gravity of the

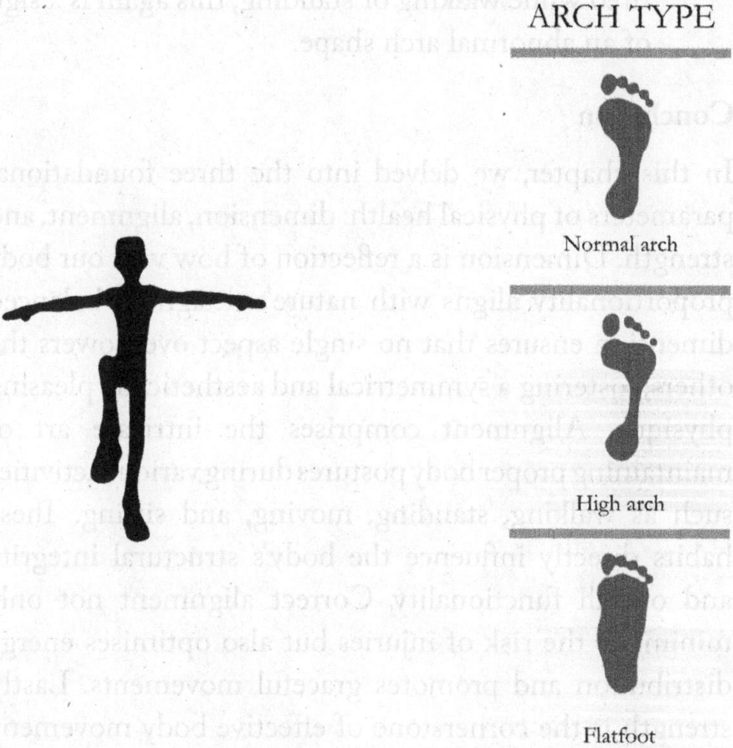

earth, then this too can lead to muscle and joints disorders or pain, if prolonged. If the arch is more or less than the normal arch shape, your feet will not be aligned while walking and will make you prone to knee or lower back injury by stressing the wrong muscles.

Other than the wet test, the shoe sole can also indicate the type of your arch or how your feet are placed. If your shoes are unevenly rubbed and more worn towards the inner lining, this is a sign of an abnormal arch. Also, if your legs quickly get tired while walking or standing, this again is a sign of an abnormal arch shape.

Conclusion

In this chapter, we delved into the three foundational parameters of physical health: dimension, alignment, and strength. Dimension is a reflection of how well our body proportionality aligns with nature's design. A balanced dimension ensures that no single aspect overpowers the others, fostering a symmetrical and aesthetically pleasing physique. Alignment comprises the intricate art of maintaining proper body postures during various activities such as walking, standing, moving, and sitting. These habits directly influence the body's structural integrity and overall functionality. Correct alignment not only minimises the risk of injuries but also optimises energy distribution and promotes graceful movements. Lastly, strength is the cornerstone of effective body movement. Coordinated muscles are essential for executing any action, and their strength dictates the fluidity and efficiency of these movements. When muscles lack the necessary strength, the body's equilibrium falters, leading to imbalances and misalignment. Thus, building and maintaining muscle strength is crucial for a healthy and functional physique. You can take the strength test by simply getting up from a cross-legged sitting posture on the floor without using any support. If you require more than two supports to stand up, it indicates a lack of strength of coordinated muscles. Alternatively, you can try standing on each leg for 30 seconds without any support.

These interconnected aspects collectively define the equilibrium and well-being of our bodies in achieving optimal physical health. For instance, weakness in strength can destabilise alignment, while poor alignment can hinder dimension proportionality. To achieve overall physical health, a harmonious balance across all three parameters is imperative. But how does one naturally achieve these physical health parameters? The following chapter will delve extensively into strategies for maintaining a body that adheres naturally to nature's design, harmonising with the gravitational forces, and cultivating the strength needed for coordinated movements.

Chapter VI

The Best Dish

'Eating right is a form of self-respect.'

Once a king announced a cooking contest in his fiefdom and proclaimed that he would award gold coins to the person who prepared the best dish. Many well-renowned chefs participated in the contest. They prepared a wide variety of food made from unique herbs, exotic vegetables, dry fruit, all kinds of meats, and whatnot.

On the day of the judgement, all the dishes were presented to the king and as he was tasting them one by one, he noted that one of the contestants—a very poor peasant—was sitting alone in a corner with a vessel covered by a dirty piece of cloth.

The king reached out and asked him, 'What are you doing here, dear peasant?'

'My Lord, I have also prepared a dish for you,' he answered. Everyone in the court was surprised by his reply and started laughing at him.

'Do you think you could compete with such professional chefs?' the king asked.

'I am not sure, my lord. But one thing is for sure that my dish is the best dish.'

The peasant's conviction stunned the king. 'Oh, is that so? Okay, show me then what have you brought.' The peasant removed the cloth covering the vessel and the king took a peek inside.

'What is this, dear peasant? It is empty. Where is the dish?'

'No, my lord. It is not empty. It is full of fresh air from my farms.' The king was taken aback. There was pin-drop silence in the court. The peasant continued, 'Yes, my lord. All the dishes you have tasted until now, you can live without them for weeks. But without my dish, you cannot live beyond a minute. Just imagine, my lord, the value of a dish without which a healthy and energetic body dies within seconds.'

The king kept listening to him intently. 'My lord, I accept that as compared to other dishes in the contest, my dish does not have any taste, no aroma, and is not as presentable. But can that be the reason for it not being considered the best dish? Just close your eyes, my lord, and breathe the air of my fields from this vessel, taste the best dish on the planet ever,' the peasant said.

'You are right, my friend,' said the king and hugged the poor peasant. 'Your dish is the best dish not only in this competition but on Mother Nature's menu too.'

***

The above story depicts the importance of air and how vital it is when it comes to sustaining life. It carries the most essential nutrients, energises the body, and eliminates waste, toxins, bacteria, and viruses. It calms the brain and stabilises the nervous system. Even a marginal depletion in the body can affect the efficiency of the heart and weaken the immune, digestive, and respiratory systems as well as cause fatigue, impact memory, fluctuate blood pressure, and initiate joint and muscle pains. Studies also show that low oxygen levels can drive cancer growth. It also has a significant impact on our mental health and emotions.

In the value chain of the ecosystem, its presence is so essential that without it, oceans will evaporate and life on earth will cease to exist. It is not merely the lifeline of living beings, but also the lifeline of the planet.

And even after knowing the importance of air in matters related to health, no one teaches us how to breathe correctly. Parents do not teach children, schools do not have it as part of their curriculum, doctors never prescribe a treatment that includes breathing, and no gym instructor trains you in breathing techniques.

The fact that breathing is an essential ingredient for good health is not new information. Many forms of yoga and meditation are based on it and also preach its importance. Now, through the aid of science, we know for a fact that breathing plays a crucial role when it comes to feeling relaxed, calm, agile, and having enhanced concentration. Yet many of us are unaware of this fact and continue to breathe unconsciously. In this chapter, we will understand how breathing in a correct manner can improve our well-being and overall health.

***

We have already covered above the importance of breathing correctly. But the quality of the air we inhale also plays a crucial role when it comes to health and well-being. And with the exponential growth of industrialisation and unprecedented rise in global transportation, the particles generated through effluvium, smoke, and dust are now part of the air, disturbing the fresh air equation and making it unhealthy to breathe. These particulates are so tiny that they are not visible to the naked eye and can easily escape through the body filtration process and mingle in our bloodstream. Also, since the polluted air has more carbon, the lungs get less oxygen and more carbon, which has a cascading effect on the entire body system.

But an interesting point to note here is that though the AQI has only deteriorated in recent times, as per the National Oceanic and Atmospheric Administration (NOAA), the data collected from three glacial cycles shows that the PM level was as high as the 200-level mark about 40 million years ago. This means that polluted air is not a new phenomenon, and it plays only a partial role when it comes to our health and the more important factor is the way we breathe. Knowing a little bit of science here would help us to substantiate the role of breathing when it comes to health.

The oxygen inhaled by our bodies is used to oxidise fat and break it into its subsequent components: carbon dioxide and water. And just as a barbecue requires a sufficient amount of air to oxidise coal, in order to burn the deposited fat, the body needs adequate oxygen. But the most amazing fact to note here is that during this process, only 16 per cent of fat converts into water and the whopping 84 per cent becomes carbon dioxide gas, which we release out through our lungs and nose. Simply put, the majority of our body fat is excreted through the process of breathing and the rest is excreted through fluids. For example, if a body loses 5 kg weight, 4.2 kg of the weight will be excreted through the nose in the form of carbon dioxide and the rest (800 grams) will be excreted through perspiration.

What this means is that by simply breathing correctly, we can extract extra fat, manage the body dimensions and overall weight, and more importantly, optimise body functioning. It also means that exercises and activities such as yoga, which lead to an increase in heart rate, are natural forms of extricating fat from the body. We will learn more about these in the subsequent chapter.

Renowned American scientist and physicist, Sheldon Saul Hendler, echoes this sentiment in his book, *The Oxygen Breakthrough*: 'Breathing is unquestionably the single most important thing you do in your life. By just breathing correctly, you can improve your health and life.'

Since now we know the importance of breathing, the next important question to consider is: How does one breathe more naturally and adequately? But before we answer this, we will need to understand the fundamentals of breathing. For many of us, breathing is a silent act performed by the subconscious mind. We simply inhale air and exhale it instantly without holding it in our lungs, which is enough to sustain ourselves, but not effective enough to be in the pink of health. So, in order to optimise our breathing, we need the participation of the active mind. In other words, we need to breathe more consciously. It is said that breathing with a conscious mind is a form of meditation. Since we have established the precursor to breathing correctly, now let's look at the various steps involved.

4-4-4 Technique

The 4-4-4 technique is divided into the following three stages:

1. Inhale for 4 seconds
2. Hold for 4 seconds
3. Exhale for 4 seconds

Start by placing one hand on your chest and the other one just below your rib cage. Then close your eyes, completely relax yourself, and breathe normally. Next, notice the movement of your hands with each breath. The important thing to remember here is that only the hand on your stomach should move while the hand on your chest should remain as still as possible. This implies that you are breathing correctly (also referred to as nose breathing).

There's another way you can check if you are breathing adequate air. Set a stopwatch for a minute, and just breathe naturally for a minute and count the total number of breaths you take in that span of time. According to research, normal breathing volume ranges from 12 to 14 breaths per minute and people with chronic heart disease tend to breathe 15 to 18 breaths per minute. Taking less than 12 breaths is a sign of good health and it also indicates that the body has a high tolerance to carbon dioxide, which translates into being able to hold your breath for a longer time. Holding your breath beyond 40 seconds indicates excellent physical endurance. If a person can't hold their breath for even 20 seconds, it signifies breathing impairment and poor physical tolerance while between 20-40 seconds reflects moderate tolerance but a propensity for heart disorders.

A common myth when it comes to breathing is that taking bigger breaths through your mouth allows you to inhale more oxygen. The fact is that deep and slow nose breathing eliminates more carbon dioxide from the lungs and distributes oxygen efficiently to all body parts through blood. Also, the nose is designed to emit and absorb oxygen directly into the blood as compared to the mouth, since the mouth is not designed to filter air. Mouth breathing also dries saliva and can lead to gingivitis, gum diseases, bad breath, gas, stomach infections, acid reflux, and even facial deformities, misaligned teeth, tongue, and lips, and uneven bite grip in children. Among adults, crooked teeth and frequent dry mouth are symptoms of mouth breathing. Overbreathing and mouth breathing also increase snoring and affect sleep quality.

Apart from the key pointers discussed above—breathing more consciously and taking moderate breaths—allow yourself access to fresh air, since our routines are confined to non-ventilated rooms that force us to re-breathe used air. This is one of the prime reasons for getting sick often. Always keep a window or a door open, even in an air-conditioned room. Make it a habit to inhale fresh air and keep track of air quality. Early morning and late evening hours in urban cities are unhealthy to walk since pollutants settle during these hours and therefore, the AQI numbers during these times are highest in the entire day. Also, living around dense traffic zones makes us highly prone to the risks of catching pollution-related diseases. A recent study published in the Lancet Medical Journal showed that people living near busier roads develop a higher risk of inflammation leading to cardiovascular and diabetes due to air pollutants.

Pollution is growing at an unprecedented rate and poses a serious threat to humanity. It is estimated that by 2050, it will be one of the major causes of death in India and China. Thus, it is important to develop a habit of using masks in polluted areas. You can also monitor pollution levels, download air quality apps, keep fresh air cans handy, install an air quality monitor at home, keep your home dust-free, and grow and keep indoor plants. Other recommended practices include living closer to greener patches and spending more time in nature. You can also practise holding your breath and extending your holding duration with time. Another thing to keep in mind is to exercise in open or well-ventilated gyms rather than in a closed AC room. So, before you select a gym, check its ventilation before you check its equipment.

Remember, our life begins and ends with a breath. But most of us remain unaware of this simple yet crucial aspect of our lives. Thus, it is critical to learn the correct form of breathing and include various breathing exercises in our day-to-day lives in order to achieve healthy and holistic living.

Chapter VII

The Best Medicine

'Pure water is the world's first and foremost medicine.'
— Slovakian proverb

Water is an essential element to propagate and sustain life. And when it comes to human health and well-being, its significance can never be overstated. Water makes up two-thirds of the human body. It carries numerous nutrients and minerals to every cell of the body, removes toxins, keeps the skin young, delays wrinkles, and cushions and lubricates joints and spinal cords. It also maintains the digestive system, strengthens immunity, and protects the body against diseases.

And today, like air pollution, water pollution has also become a global crisis. Factors such as the expansion of economic and industrial activities, intensification of usage of chemicals and synthetic substances, and increase in discharge of waste material into water bodies have led to this troubling rise in water pollution which, in turn, is causing severe harm to the health of countless people across the globe. In this chapter, we will look at the health challenges that humanity is facing due to the rise in water pollution and how we can transcend them. But first, let's understand the best practices to keep in mind when it comes to water consumption.

When and How Much to Drink

Since two-thirds of our body is made up of water, we need to make sure that it is replenished through our diet. By design, if our diet lacks the required water content, the body demands water by feeling thirsty more often. At the same time, drinking too much water unnecessarily dilutes stomach acids and blood and overworks the kidneys for no reason. Moreover, drinking water sporadically or excessively adds to body weight. So, if dry lips and dark yellow urine indicate dehydration, then colourless urine indicates over-hydration which is also unhealthy. A study shows that drinking water when our body does not need it makes it harder for us to swallow, as the brain does not regulate thirst when our body has sufficient water intake. The only time when one should drink water even when not feeling thirsty is early in the mornings as it intensifies metabolism and cleansing processes and leads to smoother bowel movement.

Another important thing to keep in mind is that as per our body design, the water needs to flow into the stomach and not directly fall into it. Meaning, that water should flow from the sidewalls as it allows the body to prepare and handle it more efficiently. Even if you're extremely thirsty, never drink with your chin angled beyond ninety degrees to your neck. Just keep the glass or the bottle straight and never let it go beyond eye level. Another good habit is to drink water slowly and in moderate quantities. This is because drinking excessive quantities of water after longer intervals does not satisfy the body's water requirements. The body simply throws the extra water out or stores it, leading to weight gain.

The above-mentioned practices have been part of human civilisation since its beginning. Our ancestors had only two ways to get their water requirement: through food and natural water bodies. So, when they chewed vegetables and fruit (which are largely made up of water), the fluid was squeezed slowly and it flowed smoothly into the stomach. Also, our ancestors never had the privilege of drinking water from taps or in glasses. Instead, they had to drink water from lakes and rivers due to which they had no other option but to sit beside the water body to drink. That is the only logic against not drinking water while standing. It does not matter what position you are in while drinking. The myth that eating or drinking while standing or in a certain position may harm the body is debatable but what's important is that the body posture should be straight or in a resting position. Eating or drinking with a slouch compresses organs that affect the overall digestive system.

Another aspect when it comes to water is when should we have it—during, after, or before meals? Like any other food, water has its digestion cycle. Water requires 5 to 120 minutes to get fully absorbed in the blood and then passes out as urine. So, the amount of water absorbed depends upon the type of meal consumed and its digestion cycle. An average meal of Indian bread, lentils, and vegetables, if chewed properly, takes around an hour to digest. If a diet contains fat, meat, and trans fats, it is ideal to drink water at least two hours before or when the body demands it. If we drink too much water with our meals, it can delay digestion as it dissolves the stomach acids. Also, probable reasons why we might have the urge to drink during a meal are:

1. The body is not receiving adequate water before eating.
2. Food is not being chewed properly.

Another important point to note is that Indian meals contain more unsaturated fats which freeze below room temperature and drinking chilled or refrigerated water after meals further delays the digestion process and does not allow the body to absorb the necessary nutrients.

Are We Drinking Healthy Water?

In its natural course, water travels through soil, rocks, and plant roots before it merges with streams, rivers, lakes, and wells. However today, it is piped through fabricated channels before it gets stored in overhead tanks and hence, it lacks the therapeutic nutrients and minerals which it attained from rocks, roots, and soil. Also, industrialisation has played a major role in the production of large quantities of harmful elements such as lead and mercury that seep deep into the earth and pollute the groundwater which is our main source of water.

So, when the urgency to clean impurities became a

necessity, home filters came into existence which was followed by the RO process with filtration technologies like UV and UF. However, these technologies remove all essential minerals from the water as well. Meaning, they made water safe to drink but also low in mineral content.

As mentioned, clean water is safe to drink but not healthy and the lack of minerals in water can lead to weakness and fatigue. Thus, there was a rise in demand to re-mineralise water. Sea salt was a great option as it was convenient to produce but soon, better options like rock salt emerged which were way more efficient when it came to enriching water with the necessary minerals. Simply adding less than half a spoon of rock salt to a litre of water can replenish the minerals lost during the filtration process and keep the body energetic throughout the day. Apart from this, there are many other healthy alternatives available such as alkaline water and the upcoming chapter will cover these aspects in more detail. Overall, the main takeaway from this section should be that we should have clean and mineral-rich water.

Conclusion

This chapter cannot be concluded without mentioning another critical role of water in human life which we haven't discussed and that is bathing. Bathing is not merely a body-cleansing activity; in reality, it holds a therapeutic value. Taking a shower with cold water activates the organs and improves the digestive system. This is why many of us feel hungry after bathing. However, it's important to note that when the organs are already active after a meal, taking a bath is not recommended as it can disrupt the digestion process. The shock of cold water can elevate the heart rate, boost blood circulation, and increase the breathing rate, resulting in a sense of alertness and freshness. Washing your face frequently with cold water throughout the day keeps the mind active. Developing a habit of washing your face every time you visit the washroom helps maintain a natural glow on your face. In short, the use of cold water contributes to building resilience against illnesses, enhancing immunity, promoting healthy and radiant skin, and making hair shinier and smoother.

Chapter VIII

The Best Match

'The simple rule of eating right is to eat, what is designed for you to eat.'

When it comes to holistic health, it is imperative for humans to nurture their relationship with nature, especially when it comes to our eating habits. But if we continue to be ignorant of our compatibility with nature and what it has to offer and instead increase our reliance on synthetic and processed products, then ill health is guaranteed. As we studied if the body's first relation is with the mind, then the second is with mother nature. If these two are managed well, good health is undeniable. Therefore, it is important for us to understand and accept how we are designed and our connection with nature which, in turn, can help us establish health principles for lifelong wellness.

So, let's first understand what our bodies reveal about our eating dispositions after which we will analyse the prominent food ingredients and their relation to our health.

What Does Our Anatomy Reveal?

Classifying humans as herbivores or carnivores as per our anatomy has always been a controversial topic among historians, anthropologists, and ecologists. Yet, if we compare and contrast our anatomical features with those of other animals, we will find many parallels to herbivore creatures. For example, our hand design, nail shape, jaw structure, and tooth sharpness do not bear the ability to kill any living organism. Apart from that, we also lack the swiftness and energy required to kill like carnivores. We have low canine teeth and flat molars in order to chew food, which is comparable to other herbivores who also chew their food in order to digest it. On the other hand, carnivores have sharp front teeth for tearing the flesh and have no molar teeth for grinding as they swallow non-chewed food. Some of the other features where we resemble herbivore characteristics are as follows.

Carnivores have relatively bigger mouths compared to their heads, whereas herbivores have relatively smaller mouths than their heads. Herbivores sip and suck water, whereas carnivores lap water. The intestinal length of a carnivore is three times its body length so that non-chewed flesh can be processed and passed through quickly. Whereas, in herbivores, it is 10 to 12 times the body length, as the food can stay longer without decaying in the intestinal tract. Herbivores also produce close to 10 times less hydrochloric acid (the acid generated in the stomach during digestion) than carnivores. Carnivores have no skin pores and perspire through their tongue while herbivores do so through their body pores. Carnivores generate their own vitamin C, whereas herbivores obtain it from their diet. So, we can see that many of our anatomical features fall in the category of herbivores.

This debate has been a controversial one due to a common myth that the vegetarian diet is not a balanced diet and lacks the adequate nutrients which our body needs. This claim has been proved wrong by several studies. The fact is that we can live exclusively on plant-based food and derive every ingredient of our daily diet from vegetarian foods. Our frame, muscles, bones, skin, nails, teeth, vision, vision, etc., all have the ability to thrive in a fleshless dietary system.

The reason for analysing which diet is optimum for us is important because diet plays a crucial role when it comes to our health and well-being. Having a compatible diet helps the body to perform multiple chemical reactions and metabolic reactions as well as effectively absorb nutrients and supply blood to all parts of the body. On the contrary, when we feed our body nutrients which are not compatible with it or cannot be digested, the body either reacts negatively or has to work harder to digest them and due to this toll, it becomes diseased.

Limitations of Human Science

Due to an unprecedented advancement of the medical field, today we have in-depth knowledge of health science and related facilities which we could have never dreamt of a few decades back. We can measure and monitor every vital health sign in a simple and quick manner. For example, just through a few simple steps, we can instantly check our cholesterol and hemoglobin levels or the amount of sodium in our body. But even though all these advancements in the field of medical science have made it easy to monitor our health vitals, the important question is whether they have really made managing our health simpler and more convenient. Another important question here is whether all the knowledge accumulated over the past few years has given the common man a better understanding of health. Let's see how complicated the subject of health can be through an example.

It is widely accepted that the ideal value for daily calorie intake can be found by simply multiplying the body weight by 22. For example, if the body weight is 68kg, then the average calorie intake would fall around 1496 (68*22) calories in a day for an average person. Additionally, people with an active job or young mothers with active children can consume 20 per cent more calories while people who do intense exercise can push their calorie consumption by 25-30 per cent. Science also says that protein and carbohydrates both contain 4 calories per gram, while fat provides 9 calories per gram. Based on these portions, a body demanding 1500 calories in a day, assuming the 40-30-30 ratio, will need:

- (1500*40%)/4 = 150gm of carbohydrate
- (1500*30%)/4 = 112gm of proteins
- (1500*30%)/9 = 50gm of fats

Thus, for a body to reduce a kilogram of weight in a month, it will have to burn an extra 288 calories every day for 30 days regularly, which can be achieved through either decreasing food consumption or by increasing physical activities/exercise. Though these simple set of equations provide us with a clear calorie intake value that one needs to follow in order to lose weight, the main issue is that there is no equation that is capable of accurately determining and tracking an individual's total daily calorie intake and expenditure in their daily routine. This is because life is complex and not every aspect of it can be confined to simple equations.

This issue also persists when it comes to knowing the amount of carbs, proteins, fats, minerals, and vitamins content in our meals. Though there are some guidelines and tools that can be applied to get a rough figure about the food ingredient, we can never get a precise figure due to the innumerable variables involved in the process.

So, does this mean there is no way we can never take charge of our eating habits and overall health as there is no precise way of calculating the exact content of our meals and their amount? Even though this is true, if one simply follows nature's principles discussed in the book, our health will fall into place by itself.

In the subsequent section, we will explore a few prime food ingredients and their effect on our health. We will also look into things to keep in mind in order to make better decisions when it comes to consuming these items.

Understanding Common Diet Elements

- **Fruits and Vegetables**

  Since ancient times, people have been well aware of the medicinal and nutritional values of fruits and vegetables and even now, the world is yet to name any disease caused by fruits and vegetables and our bodies innately know this fact. There have been numerous studies that show that eating vegetables and fruits increases happiness levels because the mind knows they are the best sources of nutrients and feels no guilt about eating them. Moreover, researchers have found that people who changed their diet from almost having no fruits and vegetables to eight portions a day significantly transformed their health within 24 months.

  But the luxury of eating fresh fruits and vegetables has been gradually reducing as most populations live far away from the sources where these food items are procured. It is estimated that the nutrient value of a produce drops to as low as 40 per cent within 4 to 24 hours from the time it is plucked. Thus, we can see that the freshness of the harvest depends on the distance it has to travel before it reaches your plate. Additionally, the temperature and several other condition fluctuations between territories further hamper the nutrient content.

  There are some measures we can take to overcome this issue. Local markets are a good source of fresh, locally grown produce. The produce available in such markets is not only fresh but also economical as compared to imported produce.

Another important thing to keep in mind is the design feature of fruits and vegetables, which indicates the way that particular item should be eaten. Potatoes, carrots, radishes, cucumbers, ladyfingers, and brinjals can be eaten with the skin as the skin carries several essential nutrients. On the other hand, oranges, bananas, lychees, peas, onions, and garlic are eaten without the skin by design. Also, when you eat a whole fruit, you can consume both the juices and fibre together. If you leave the fibre aside and just drink juice, then it is like a sugar attack and the insulin will have to dilute it. In such a scenario, even fruits can propagate diabetes. Also, drinking fruit juice instead of eating the fruit skips aspects such as chewing, biting, and mixing saliva which is essential when it comes to consuming fibre. Some people even grind fruit into pulp. It is fair to do so for the sick people who are not in a position to chew and swallow. However, if you can, why not eat the whole fruit?

- **Cereal and Grains**

Grains weren't a part of the diet for the vast majority of human history and only appeared in the last 6000 years with the advent of organised farming. As for their nutritional value, they are a great source of carbohydrates and protein as well as vitamins and minerals. They also help in maintaining blood levels and reduce the risk of developing diseases such as diabetes, colon cancer, and coronary heart disease.

However, with the onset of food processing in the last 100 years or so, the quality of grains has been significantly impacted. Until now we have been eating wholegrain food, i.e., with all three parts: bran, germ and endosperm. Bran is the outer part of the grain and is called fibre, the germ is the seed of the grain and contains nutrients along with antioxidants, and the endosperm is the pulp that contains carbohydrates and proteins.

But refined flour, what we mostly eat, is without bran and germ, which makes it highly rich in carbohydrates. Most food labels provide misleading messaging with terms like 'whole-germ' or 'whole-meal' as this does not mean that the product contains all three components of the grain. Till the late nineties, the household trend used to be to buy wholegrain flour for its health benefits but due to adulteration and high sugar content, it led to a surge of diabetes and other health-related issues.

Numerous studies have shown that people who eat wholegrain food, mainly wheat and oats, have a lower risk of diabetes, obesity, and heart disease and live longer. On the other hand, when we eat refined grains, our sugar level increases rapidly and then drops quickly. And when it drops, we intend to feel hungry again and therefore, we end up eating more, leading to high sugar levels and obesity.

The core issue here is the processing of the grains as it removes the healthiest part of the grain, which elicits a greater insulin response to dissolve sugar, whereas the wholegrain substitute leads to significantly less insulin release. Practically put, it is wise to buy atta (flour) in a smaller quantity of 5 to 10 kilograms and eat it fresh. The term fresh here not only means freshly ground but also the freshness of the seasonal wheat. By doing do so, we can avail all the health-supportive aspects of wholegrain food.

- **Meat**

As discussed earlier, by design, humans are herbivores but there is plenty of evidence that shows that our ancestors hunted animals and lived on animal meat. Humans are the only creatures that eat cooked meat. And with growing demand, animal farming has adopted ways to produce quicker and uses an infestation of chemicals for a fresh and pink look. Moreover, it is 5 to 6 times more expensive than the average vegetable and takes more time and fuel to cook and even more time to digest. Moreover, the stomach does not generate enough hydrochloric acid to digest meat and thus, it remains and decays within the digestive system for days before it is flushed.

With the increasing demand for meat globally, the raising of livestock has become a major concern for the environment and is becoming a major hazard to human health. Livestock farming produces more greenhouse gas emissions than all oil transportation put together. The rising appetite for meat agriculture and production is not only making it accessible to more people but is also a major contributor to climate change. By bringing meat consumption to the recommended level, the livestock for meat and dairy products will reduce drastically and coupled with a paradigm shift in dietary change, will not reduce only emissions levels across the globe, but also reduce heart diseases and cancer. Just controlling livestock farming will protect our health and the climate from catastrophic dangers. If we treat animals like nations, protect them and refuse to consume meat, there will be peace all around and no one will starve or get sick enough to the level of demanding hospitalisation.

- **Sugar**

It is a well-known fact that if sugar alone is controlled in the diet, most people will become healthy. And in current times, sugar, which is a carbohydrate, is the main culprit when it comes to obesity and overall health deterioration. And the reason why sugar has become ubiquitous in the food industry is that it is exceptionally delicious and highly addictive. The main cause why we crave sugar is because the consumption of sugar produces the same acid in the brain as cocaine or sex.

When we eat sugar, our body has two options, either burn it for energy or convert it into fat which can be stored by the body. But due to its excessive presence in all kinds of foods, our consumption of sugar has increased manifold. In fact, the sugar molecule can even be found in the same product in 2-3 different forms which leads to the customer misinterpreting the amount of sugar in that product.

To control sugar, it is important to understand its relationship with insulin. Whenever the body consumes high amounts of sugar, the brain sends a signal to the pancreas to take stock of the amount of sugar and release insulin to mix with the sugar and dilute it. Insulin is one of the most important acids, and things like exercising and good eating habits can help the body produce insulin efficiently. But the more sugar in the blood, the higher the demand for insulin and the more insulin, the more sugar the body demands. Thus, we can see how unmitigated sugar intake can turn into an ever-going vicious cycle.

To overcome this 21st-century menace, by simply controlling the level of sugar ingestion, half the battle is won. It is also important to be able to differentiate two forms of sugar: natural and non-natural. Non-natural sugar denotes all the artificial forms of sugar while natural sugar refers to sugar variants derived from organic sources. So, when the body consumes sugar through organic sources such as fruits, it also consumes a lot of fibre, vitamins, and minerals. This is the reason having a fruit does not affect the sugar level as much as unnatural sugar because the fibre content controls the sugar attack and avoids the demand for extra insulin.

To recap all the essential points covered so far:

- Our body requires complex and natural nutrients in moderate quantities. Anything excessive metabolises quickly, resulting in rapid spikes or drops in the body matrix.
- Control table sugar or artificial sugar intake or avoid it completely.
- Every time you buy processed food, remember how it may negatively affect your health and the health of your family.
- Natural sugar found in organic sources such as natural jaggery or powdered jaggery are healthy substitutes and their taste is similar to white sugar.

- **Salt**

Salt was used as a preservative and gradually, over the years, became a part of our diet. But it can be so harmful that in ancient times, salt overdose was preferred for suicide. Even the death penalties were carried out with the use of salt.

Most health experts recommend limiting salt intake to no more than 6g per day for an average person and lower in cases of people with high blood pressure, diabetes, or kidney disease. Thus, being mindful of salt intake and choosing healthier alternatives can help promote better health and reduce the risk of certain health conditions. Nowadays, many processed and packaged foods contain high amounts of sodium, even if they don't taste salty. Ready-to-eat snacks and chips carry raw and sea salt, which presents the danger of hypertension, heart disease, and osteoporosis. Therefore, it's important to look out for the mention of 'low sodium', 'reduced sodium,', or 'no added salt' on the food labels.

It is a good habit to use salt as a luxury item and experiment with other herbs, spices, and flavourings to add taste to your meals without relying on salt. Additionally, avoid putting salt on the table, as this can increase overall sodium intake. Also, be mindful of using substitutes as some salt substitutes are made with potassium chloride, which can be harmful to people on medication or with certain medical conditions, such as kidney disease. More importantly, stay hydrated. Drinking plenty of water can help flush excess sodium out of the body and maintain a healthy fluid balance.

- **Milk**

  Well, milk is the most controversial element of our present-day diet. There have been sharp arguments both in favour and opposition about whether it is good or bad for health. Let us look at some objective facts to understand this debate better.

  Biologically, milk is necessary for a creature as long as their mother feeds them but humans are the only species that drink the milk of other animals and even beyond their childhood phase. But we don't have sufficient evidence to convincingly judge whether this is a good or bad practice.

  One of the major points is that milk is highly rich in protein but the question that arises here is whether we need such a high quantity of protein. If we look at the composition, human milk contains 1g of protein as compared to 3.6g per 100 grams of cow milk, which is 2.5 times more protein than we need and consuming something more than our body needs can have an adverse effect on overall health. Another point to note here is that with the rising demands of milk consumption, cows and buffaloes are forcibly impregnated and medically manipulated to produce up to 12 times the usual milk they would have naturally produced to feed a calf. Moreover, adding preservatives and steps such as pasteurisation significantly impact the nutritional value of processed milk. Some studies have also found that milk carries hormones which can result in skin acne, early puberty, and breast and prostate cancer in children. Milk from other animals can also disrupt the hormonal system. If a person is experiencing acne, pre-menstrual syndrome or PCOS, gastrointestinal problems, or unwanted hair growth, minimising or completely eliminating milk from the diet may help. Switching to plant-based milk like coconut, soy, almond, or low-fat milk is also recommended as it carries a low number of hormones.

- **Oil**

  Cooking oils are again among the most used items the world over, but they are particularly not beneficial for health. Mostly because it is that it has no pH value as there is no water in it. For example, Canola seeds, which are not seeds in the first place, are processed with a petroleum solvent to extract oil, and then the extra wax is removed with the chemicals and eventually deodorised to improve the product's smell and make it edible. Another danger in consuming processed items is the lack of knowledge about the quality of the ingredients, the processes involved, and the use of chemicals while processing.

When it comes to fats, there is still no unanimous consensus on whether unsaturated fats or saturated fats are good for health, but trans-fats found in deep-fried foods are definitely unhealthy. Several studies show that ghee, coconut, and mustard oil are better options since

> they contain both fats (unsaturated and saturated) in good proportions. And even though oil brands continue to lure consumers, the fact remains that unsaturated and saturated fats in the natural form are a superior choice.
>
> Olive oil is believed to be the queen of oils, though its nutrient value often varies with different variants. Extra virgin oil is rich and edible, but it is not meant for cooking. It is a cold-pressed oil without any chemical reaction and carries a natural green colour and aroma. Refined olive oil is used for very light cooking and is slightly lower in nutrient value, similar to other vegetable oils.

To summarise, knowing these ingredients alone will not help you to be smart and healthy. Moreover, we have known for a long time now the harmful effects of sugar, salt, and fat, yet more and more people are consuming them in excessive quantities every day. So, if every other ingredient is unhealthy to eat, then what should we do? We will explore this in the coming chapters.

Chapter IX

The Best Way

'In the eternal fight between pleasure and self-control, the victor decides our health.'

So far, we have explored several health principles and how the prevalence of unhealthy ingredients in food items is contributing to a health crisis on a global scale. The truth is that we are not eating as per our design and perhaps need to completely alter our lifestyle but that might not be practically possible and easy to accomplish, seeing how deeply we are entrenched in the modern ways of life. Therefore, it is important to find a balance between adhering to these principles while still enjoying modern food options to feel both healthy and happy. While a diet rich in fruits and vegetables is widely acknowledged as the best way to live healthily, it's essential to recognise that our lifestyle habits, eating choices, and exercise routines are constantly evolving. Also, we enjoy flavourful food and indulging in drinks and meals that aren't inherently designed for us. As stated in the preface, this book aims to bridge the gap between natural principles and our contemporary ways of living and eating. In this chapter, we will explore ways to relish our favourite dishes while remaining healthy and look into powerful concepts and scientific rules to simplify healthy eating. So, now let's begin with the science of SMART eating.

* * *

FIT Principle: Control your Tongue

Hunger is a major component of our diet but there are two types of hunger—physical and mental hunger. Physical hunger relates to our bodies asking for food while mental hunger relates to our mind asking for food. Another important difference between the two is that our physical hunger gets satiated when we are full but with mental hunger, the mind can crave more food even when the stomach is full. And it is due to this mind eating habits that overeating and obesity have become a global problem.

Eating something just because it is handy, overloading the plate with more than you can eat, eating dessert after a heavy meal, or munching something or the other in between the meals are some of the signs when a 'feel' takes over 'fact'. The important factor here is that in all of the cases mentioned, the body suffers because we lack control over the tongue. And we get so consumed by the taste of food that we start deceiving ourselves by saying that it is occasional and that a little candy, a small piece of chocolate, a small scoop of ice cream, a single bite of a burger, or a few sips of a cold drink cannot do much harm. But now imagine the impact a tiny medicine pill can have on our body. This means that even a small dosage of a substance can have drastic effects on our body and this applies to everything we eat. Also, all major food manufacturing companies are well aware of this fact and make food items that exploit the weakness of the tongue.

Hence, it is important that we let fact get the upper hand over feel and this is only possible if we become more conscious of the role our tongue plays when it comes to our eating habits. We all know that a glass of aerated water has as much as 23 sachets of artificial sugar. We know that raw salt sprinkled over the chips is a slow poison and contains empty calories. We know that deep-fried snacks are the most dangerous fats, which the body does not need. We know that ice creams carry artificial sweeteners which are harmful to our bodies. This is where we need to control our feelings and strengthen our ability to say 'No' to food we should not eat. Simply put, we need to develop the courage to say no to bad eating habits and say yes to health.

This aspect of gaining control of our tongue is a fight against the mind. Our mind has the propensity to be unstoppable; it will wander in the future-high, but the tongue needs to be in the present-neutral to make wise decisions. In other words, it is also our duty to let our mind know that we are in charge and make decisions that will reap long-term health benefits. But the complete blame can't be put on the tongues alone'; we need to teach it when to say 'yes' or 'no', and this is only the way we can have better control over what to eat and what not to.

pH: The Indicator of Health

Humans have invented a scientific indicator that clearly demarcates what is healthy and what is unhealthy, but unfortunately, it is used rarely. In fact, this simple parameter is the father of all health statistics and acts as a quality marker for other practices apart from eating, such as cooking and farming, and also reveals the quality aspect of things including water, air, soil, blood, urine, etc. And this indicator is called the potential of hydrogen and is denoted by the symbol, pH.

The term pH was originally defined in 1909 by a Danish biochemist and Nobel laureate, Soren Peter Lauritz Sorenson. In scientific definition, it indicates the ions of hydrogen in a fluid. And the higher the number of ions in a fluid, the more acidic the solution will be and vice versa. So, every time we consume a food item, the body's metabolic processes produce an enormous number of acids to digest food and distribute nutrients to every cell. But since our cells and tissues require a moderately alkaline environment to function properly, our body neutralises and excretes the vast majority of acids to maintain the alkaline balance at the cell level. As Albert Szent-Gyorgyi mentioned, 'The body is alkaline by design, but acidic by function.'

The important point to note here is that all metabolic processes of the body aim to preserve a suitable balance within the two basic chemical compounds, acids and alkalis. So, whether we strive to sustain daily meal-by-meal health or procure long-term good health, the balance of these compounds is of utmost essential, and even a marginal imbalance between the two can make the body susceptible to disorders, diseases, infections, flu, virus, influenza, fungus, etc. On the other hand, if we have the optimum pH balance, it makes our body feel energetic, relaxed, active, and healthy.

pH is measured on a scale of 1 to 14, where 1 represents highly acidic and 14 signifies highly alkaline. The neutral value on the pH scale is seven, which is neither acidic nor alkali and anything above a 7 on the pH level is alkaline and anything below 7 is acidic. A pH value above seven implies that the body is healthy, has a good metabolism and immune system, and is less prone to diseases. Also, the body is only vulnerable to viruses or any kind of disease only when its pH level is less than seven, i.e., it is in an acidic state.

Generally, our body maintains an average pH of 7.4. Apart from it, organs as well as blood have their own pH levels. And though pH levels of organs can vary, the blood pH level has to be precisely between 7.365 to 7.45. To put this in context, the body's pH level can descend to 5.5 and still sustain, but if the blood pH level drops to 7.0, the body dies in seconds. So, when the pH level of the blood drops down, the organs must sacrifice their pH level to preserve the blood pH level. And when the pH levels of organs get compromised, diseases like obesity, diabetes, and arthritis transpire. Thus, when a body becomes afflicted with a disease, infection, virus etc., the respective organ or part has to compromise its health to sustain the blood pH.

How Does pH Relate to Food?

A natural question that arises when on the topic of pH factor is from where acids and alkalis enter our body, and the answer is through what we eat and drink. And here again, we can use the pH levels to get to know the acid-alkaline balance of the food we eat. Now let's see how the pH levels of food affect the body.

When the body ingests anything, the digestive and metabolic processes transform it into a kind of ash, which is either alkaline or acidic, depending upon the nutrient value of that food. So, when we have too much acidic food, the kidneys act upon these metabolically produced acids in order to excrete extra acids through urine and retain the body's pH level. In addition to kidneys, the lungs help sustain the pH level of the body by serving oxygen to the blood. The blood carries oxygen, Co2, and hydrogen. Carbon dioxide (Co2) is acidic, while the other two gases are neutral on the pH scale. In an attempt to eliminate increased levels of carbonic acid, which is a sign that the body is becoming overly acidic, the body increases the respiratory rate. And as we have covered that breathing rapidly is a sign of ill health, and in scientific terms, it means that the body is in an acidic state. Let's understand this better with an example.

A glass of Coca-Cola has a pH level of 2.5 while water is a pH 7. Scientifically, this means that a glass of Coca-Cola is 50,000 times more acidic than a glass of water. Therefore, when you get a kick through Coca-Cola or alcohol, it is the body's reaction to release alkaline from the stored organs to sustain the acidic level due to high acidic ingestion. And when such practices become regular, the body is left with no option but to extricate nutrients stored in the bones and other vital tissues and use them to fight the acidic state, making the rest of the body vulnerable to infection, flu, virus, bacteria, and eventually illness and diseases. You can notice a similar phenomenon when you consume sugar. So, whenever we eat anything which is high in sugar content, we get a kick of energy, but it also makes the body more lethargic and inactive, because the body demands more energy to keep the pH in control. The same thing happens when a body consumes highly acidic foods.

Eat a Balanced Acidic-Alkaline Diet

Over the years, our internal bodies have become war zones to fight against our excessive and unhealthy eating choices. The deteriorating quality of food and desire for more comfort have drastically impacted our overall health. And this is where the pH level can guide us in making healthier eating choices.

As mentioned before, having a high acidic pH value is harmful to our body. So, does that mean that we need to solely focus on alkaline food items? The answer is 'No' as the body also becomes vulnerable to disorders when it is overly alkaline—a condition known as alkalosis. Hence, the key to good health is a balance of these two chemical compounds. The question that arises here is how we can find a balance in our alkaline and acidic food intake in the current, contemporary food market. Let's explore this.

For a body to maintain the standard pH level, it requires a balance of 80 per cent alkaline content and 20 per cent acidic content. This means we have the space to safely eat acidic food for up to 20 per cent of our daily diet. This aspect will also relieve some of your guilt about unhealthy eating. But the issue that arises here is that it is difficult to classify foods as alkaline and acidic. For this, one can use the various charts available on Google, but the chart I highly recommend is from the book, *The Acid-Alkaline Food Guide*, authored by Dr Susan E. Brown and Larry Trivieri Jr. Some of the top-ranking alkaline foods are roots, cruciferous vegetables, lemon, garlic, and capsicum while some of acidic foods include meat, eggs, and dairy products as well as items high in sugar and trans-fats content. Also, fried and processed foods are generally highly acidic.

So, in the current food culture, which is dominated by acidic foods, we need to be mindful of taking proper amounts of alkaline foods in our diet. A good habit to have is to eat alkaline accompaniments like lemon, mint, cinnamon, ginger, and coconut with acidic foods in order to regulate overall pH level. Another reason why we should put emphasise on eating alkaline foods is that alkaline foods contain fat-burning calories and have more nutrients while acidic foods carry fat-storing hormones with less nutrient value.

All in all, if you want to control your tongue—in other words, control your urge—for acidic foods and maintain a ratio of 80:20 of alkaline and acidic foods in your diet, you will be able to preserve a good pH level which in turn will make your body's immunity strong which, in turn, will protect you from disease or seasonal illness. Remember that there are no diseases which can develop in an alkaline-acidic balanced body.

Cooking the Right Way

In the above section, we covered the importance of incorporating alkaline foods in our diet but there is more to this aspect. Simply having more alkaline foods is not enough; how we have them is critically important as the way we cook food can have a significant impact on the nutrient and overall quality of food. Let's investigate some of the common misconceptions and new insights regarding best cooking practices and how they affect the pH and nutrient value of the food.

Not many would know that the most common method of cooking rice—a staple diet of most parts of the world—leaves behind arsenic particles. In a recent study, traces of arsenic were found in rice boiled in a pan. This chemical is linked to heart disease, diabetes, and cancer. The study also suggests that soaking rice overnight followed by a 1:5 ratio for boiling and then draining the excess water reduces the level of toxins by 80 per cent. This is but one example that shows how food can be affected by the style of cooking adopted.

Deep-frying generally strips away alkaline nutrients drastically. As discussed earlier, deep-frying is done in trans-fats which are not additive to the body and are low in pH levels too. Also, it requires more metabolic energy to digest deep-fried foods and the probability of improper cooking in deep-fried oil is high since the food inside cannot be seen when it is being cooked. A study shows that half-cooked meat can lead to paralysis, which even antibiotics cannot treat. Avoiding deep-fried food is generally a good health principle, but if you enjoy eating deep-fried food, you need to balance it with foods that are more alkaline. If you are eating out, attending functions, visiting friends, or on vacation, stock your body up with alkaline foods and then pamper yourself with a fried delicacy without any guilt.

Microwave cooking is another popular form of cooking. Many studies have shown that microwave food depletes red blood cells and can even lower the heart rate. More so, alkalinity reduces in the microwave, since it is another method to heat and cook. Some alkaline-safe cooking methods include slow and indirect heat methods such as steaming, low-heat cooking, baking, boiling, simmering, and roasting. The pressure cooker is another healthy cooking option as it preserves nutrients and does not allow them to escape. Covered cooking helps restore nutrient value and vitamins up to 90-95 per cent as compared to steam cooking which restores 75-90 per cent while roasting and boiling constitute 55-90 per cent and 40-75 per cent respectively. Therefore, to avoid fat and oil in homely Indian red curries, you can boil onions, tomatoes, garlic, and ginger in water in a pressure cooker, add flavour, and cook with an open lid. It saves time and is also healthy.

Good Utensils Equals Good Health

Since utensils and cookware form an integral part of cooking and eating, it is important to know the best practices when using them. One of the foremost issues is that the metal of the utensil can leach into the food and cost us our health. Non-stick cookware has also been controversial due to the risk of toxic material used to make the product. Also, the coating of the non-stick utensils tends to break down over a period due to high heat. The scratches and chips release chemicals that leach into the food we consume and cause cancerous diseases. Thus, it is a good practice to avoid coated cookware as it is not safe for cooking. Cast iron and stainless steel are better choices to cook with, as both are not only safe but also easy to clean and are naturally non-stick. Moreover, cast iron utensils enhance the iron value of the diet and retain heat for a longer period but need dry storage to keep them safe from rusting.

Another metal used extensively for utensils manufacturing is aluminium. And though, over the years, many developments have taken place to improve aluminium cookware, it still remains considerably risky and can cause diseases like Alzheimer's. A recent study on aluminium cookware made by ten developed countries found that it reduces children's IQ levels and school performance significantly. Therefore, it is advisable to avoid high-heat cooking and use non-coated aluminium only or steel.

Utensils made of copper, though expensive, can help in fulfilling the body's need for copper (900 micrograms), carry a very low risk of toxicity, and claim to have low chances of copper leaching into the food, even for more acidic food items. But the best among all is low-cost earthen cookware. For years, it has been a part of the Indian kitchen but now has been replaced by longer-lasting metal utensils and other modern utensils. The unique quality of earthen cookware is that it is porous which allows heat and moisture to circulate, unlike metal cookware. However, the best quality of earthenware is that it is made up of clay which is alkaline in nature and normalises the pH balance of acidic food. Even highly acidic food like tomato sauce will take some natural sweetness from the clay, just as tea does from clay-based cups. However, these properties are not applicable if the earthenware is glazed with chemicals used to improve its look.

Kitchen sponges, steel brushes, and scrubbers not only can damage the surface of all utensils and contaminate them but can also become a breeding hub for harmful bacteria, yeast, and moulds. Make sure sponges and other cleaning materials are soaked in hot water after cleaning and properly dried before the next use. As mentioned, scrubbers can also scratch away the coating of utensils and make the surface pitted, thereby allowing leaching while cooking. The same stands true for chopping boards, especially with wooden surfaces. They retain moisture in between cuts on the surface and can contaminate if not cleaned and dried properly.

Timing and Sequence: Important Aspects of Healthy Eating

We have covered what to eat and how to cook, but an equally important aspect is when to eat. Each food item has a specified period for it to get processed in the stomach and then digested. This whole process runs smoothly when the food items travel at their assigned speed and are flushed out normally. Any delay in this process can lead to gastric inflammation. Also, the more fat, oil, and sugar we add to our food, the further it delays the breakdown and digestion processes. Therefore, fried or highly acidic foods should never be part of the starter or appetiser unless there is a gap of an hour before the main meal.

One of the major reasons for an unshapely midsection and improper bowel movement is not having a disciplined routine when it comes to evening meals which can also result in infections and fluctuations in the pH level of the body. Not only that, but the energy level of the next day is also dependent on this meal.

A common unhealthy eating habit consists of eating acidic foods followed by carbs and then sweets—the three-course meal—which is sure to cause an accumulation of fat around the midsection. We also normally overeat spicy foods which create inflammation and reflux in the body, leading to discomfort while sleeping. Moreover, we eat our meals mindlessly; we sit on the bed and not at the dining table, and watch TV while eating, and generally sleep within 1-2 hours of dinner. The body rests during the night and does not burn calories. That is why most Indians gain a heavy midsection and develop a weaker body.

Dinner should be only one-fourth of the total food consumed during the day and needs to be rich in alkaline foods. If your dinner includes acidic food like refined, sugary, milk, or fried food items then you should always eat an early dinner, around 7 o'clock. You can also start with vegetables, lentils, salads, and fruit first and then shift to rice and roti. This way, you will not only begin your meal by munching healthy foods but also make sure that you eat your food at the right time and in the right sequence, which matters the most when it comes to healthy eating habits.

Eat as per Your Routine

There has been confusion on whether we should eat a heavy breakfast or a heavy dinner. Many people believe that breakfast should be the full stomach meal of the day, since it is taken after a long sleep break. However, this trend does not stand true at all. During olden times, the laborious physical activity during the day demanded people to have a heavy breakfast, but the routines and lifestyles of current times are different. Simply put, we do not burn the same number of calories every day as our meal calorie intake.

If you have a sedentary routine, a few small meals with plenty of water will be a better choice than one heavy meal at lunch. If a child has PE (physical education) or some kind of physical activity such as dance on a day, then they can stock up more calories during breakfast and can also have an extra meal later to cope with the calorie burn of the day.

The point to remember here is that the body needs to adhere to a different diet every day as per the daily demand for calories. If you are skipping your exercise for a day, you should not continue with the same meal chart since you are not burning the same number of calories. The reason we fall sick quite often, even when healthy, is because we allow our pH level to fluctuate. A standard diet and the same amount of the kind of meals each day will not produce optimum results. You are unique and every day is unique and accordingly, your meal plan for the day should be adjusted as per the physical activities of the day.

Chew Your Way to Healthier Eating

Though it might not seem so, chewing plays a crucial role when it comes to maintaining good health. In fact, even a holistic and balanced diet will not give us the expected results if not chewed properly. Furthermore, improperly chewed food takes longer to digest and leads to food decay and reflux. But unfortunately, many of us normally chew mindlessly and do pay any attention to the chewing process. Nowadays, we eat our food while watching TV, chatting, reading, or thinking and do not prioritise the act of chewing. Thus, we need to be mindful of how we chew our food and regard it as equally important as any other healthy habit, such as exercising.

In the process of chewing, saliva prepares the food for digestion and also adds its pH content to it. After leaving the mouth, food rests for 2-4 hours in the stomach, depending on its nature. The typical Indian meal consists of roti, lentil, and vegetables, and since the chewing time for both is the same, the vegetables get chewed properly since it is soft and easy to chew but the roti does not get chewed properly. This leads to bloating and a delay in digestion. In fact, vegetables and roti should not be chewed together. Instead, take a bite of the roti first and chew 5-10 times, then take the vegetable and chew further together. Just ensure that the food turns into a fine and tasteless paste in the mouth before you swallow.

Examine the Packaging Labels

Today, a dream shared by many individuals is of living in the countryside where one is close to nature and consuming pure organic food. And the reason why this has become a common aspiration for many is that people see the dominance of the packaged and processed in the market propelled by profit-seeking businesses. Also, living in such fast-paced times, one has no option but to be dependent on such packed eatables and this dependency has just been increasing with time. Bread, milk, butter, yoghurt, biscuits, refined oil, flour, snacks—every food item that one can think of is coming from these companies and nothing is being homegrown. And when it comes to the quality of ingredients and the manufacturing process, one has no option but to either have blind trust or remain ignorant.

But in recent times, the public has become more conscious about what they are eating and want to know all the details relating to their food items, and this is where the packaging labels play a crucial role. As per the law, all companies have to correctly display the ingredients going into their eatables for the information of the buyers and this knowledge helps consumers decide what is right for them and what is not.

So now, all one has to do is check the packaging label and if everything looks good then that means it is a healthy product, right? The truth is more complex than that as many companies include misleading messaging and information that is deliberately twisted in order to fool the consumer and this, in turn, can lead to serious health problems. A common tactic employed by manufacturers is to lure people through by striking marketing campaigns like 'Cholesterol-Free', 'No Sugar', 'Whole Wheat', 'Fat-Free', 'New and Improved', '100% Organic', and so on. Brands manipulate and interpret food laws to mislead their consumers. Thus, it is important to not follow brands blindly and take a closer look at the products you choose. Let's look at some of the pointers on the packaging labels to be mindful about.

One of the most misleading or even confusing values on the packaging labels is the calorie count. Like most health ingredients, calories are also a topic of intense debate among health experts, and manufacturers use this to exploit their consumers. The units used for calories are 'Kcal', 'Calories', 'Cal' or 'cal', and in mathematical values, one-kilo calorie is equivalent to 1000 calories, just like one kilogram is 1000 grams. However, 'cal' and 'Cal' are not the same thing. Most manufacturers refer to 'Kcal' as 'Cal'—note the capital 'C'. If a label says '1kcal' or '1Cal', it means 1000 calories. When they mention you need to burn 1600 calories in a day, it actually means 1.6 Kcal.

Another important value to consider is fat. Some products might show the fats as 0, in case the quantity is less than one, especially in the case of trans fats, and other ingredients representing fat may be referred to as hydrogenated oil or some other form. But the thing that's not generally known is that a couple of servings of a food item with zero trans-fat will still have quite a good quantity of trans-fats. There are also some products which claim to be 'fat-free' but are loaded with sugar. Similarly, 'sugar-free' products may be full of fat. It is advisable to take note of calorie content, whenever you find the counts suspicious.

Also, be mindful of products with ingredients like beet sugar, inverted sugar, corn syrup, HFCS, sweetener and ingredients ending with 'ose' like glucose and fructose as this means that they contain sugar. In order to show a lower sugar content than the actual per serving, it is possible that different sugar ingredients are mentioned within a single product itself. Products with misleading labels like 'No sugar added' or 'Sugar-free' may not carry any of the abovementioned ingredients but may still carry sugar from carbohydrates and foods like fruits, vegetables, and milk.

Products with high quantities of fat, sugar, or sodium should generally be avoided. Choose products with around seven to eight selective ingredients at the most, as products with a lengthy list of ingredients carry preservatives and artificial flavours and colours.

Another thing which confuses a large number of people is the difference between wholegrain and multigrain and many consider them as the same thing, which is not true. While multigrain bread is a mix of refined corn, brown rice, oats, and wheat, it does not contain fibre and seed, whereas wholegrain refers to the full grain along with fibre and seed as well. Bakery bread may add a brown colour to make pure refined bread look like multigrain bread.

These are some factors that show why it is crucial to check the labels and recognise what you're consuming. It is strongly recommended to build this as a regular practice and gradually learn to distinguish between healthy and unhealthy food options, especially in the current market where everything is marketed as a healthy product. You can also take the assistance of the internet where all the relevant information pertaining to any food item can be easily found. And with the right knowledge, you will be able to make informed decisions when buying any product.

SMART Eating Principles

We have discussed multiple aspects when it comes to eating right and healthy. To put together all the principles of healthy eating in a manner that is easy to follow and remember, we can use the acronym: SMART. Each letter in this term represents a principle as given below.

- **S: Style of cooking**

  This point elucidates that baking, steaming, boiling, sautéing, and non-oily cooking are healthier cooking options as these methods better retain food nutrients and do not significantly alter the pH level of the food.

- **M: Mindful, Munching, and Moderation**

  Consciously eating and paying attention to every bite is an important aspect of eating healthy. This also prepares the body and allows for more effective and efficient digestion and utilisation of food. We have also learnt that food digestion begins in the mouth itself and the process of chewing (munching) adds enzymes to the food and makes it easier for the stomach to process it. Lastly, eat in moderation as balance is the key to good health and a good balance of acidic and alkaline is the ultimate principle of good health.

- **A: Alkaline-Acidic Balanced Diet**
  Eat more alkaline and less acidic food as chronic pH imbalance can disrupt several body systems and weaken body immunity, thereby making it vulnerable to diseases.

- **R: Routine**
  You should plan your diet as per your routine. A hectic day will require more alkaline food and a sedentary day means consuming less acidic food.

- **T: Timing and Sequence**
  The timing of our meals is crucial and ideally, we should have our meals neither too early nor too late. Additionally, the order in which we consume our meals holds equal significance. Food items with a quick digestion cycle, like fruits, curd, and salad, should be consumed first. This should be followed by vegetables, meat, and roti (Indian bread). We can easily find details pertaining to the digestion cycle of food we normally eat on the internet and consume them in the order of their digestion time.

***

The pursuit of good health is an ongoing journey, and there is another crucial aspect that can make all the difference. Dr Lynda Frassetto, an esteemed academic at the University of California, has highlighted the three sources of acidity include our dietary choices, inhaled substances, and perhaps most importantly, stress. The impact of stress on our bodies is so significant that even a single burst of adrenaline can neutralise an alkaline diet. Unfortunately, the declining quality of our food and increasing levels of professional and personal stress prevent our bodies from effectively neutralising toxins. However, by managing stress and maintaining dietary discipline, we can achieve optimal health. The question is, how can we manage stress effectively? We will explore this in the next chapter. So, let's move forward and discover how we can overcome stress and take control of our day-to-day health.

Chapter X
THE BEST HOBBY

'Good health can never be sustained in comfort zones.'

Did you know that there is a disease that is widespread among all human beings, yet it goes largely unnoticed? This disease silently impacts our health and slowly can lead to other more serious issues as well. Are you curious to know what this disease is and how we can overcome it naturally? In this chapter, we will uncover this mysterious disease and explore some new health principles and practical solutions for healthy living.

The Inconvenience of Convenience

Over the last few centuries, we have drastically transformed our surroundings. This change has been further catalysed by the rapid growth in technology and events such as the Industrial Revolution, and at the core of this transformation lies our unending desire for comfort and convenience. And though this desire of ours has not only severely affected the environment and atmosphere but also our health, we continue to accelerate on this path, wanting more convenience and more comfort.

The fact is that this craving for convenience has always been an integral part of human nature, and there are people and organisations that exploit this characteristic for their personal advantage. Just look around you and you will find many products that have been specifically designed and invented to make human life more convenient. But what is not apparent is the effect of these products on human health and nature. A great example highlighting this was the initial rise of AC usage. During this time period, ACs provided a magical solution to counter the heat, especially in hot and humid zones, which led to a significant increase in the demand for ACs. But much later, it was found out that CFCs (chlorofluorocarbons) emitted by the ACs had severely damaged the earth's ozone layer.

Moreover, the impact of chasing more and more convenience on the external world can still be gauged but its impact becomes more insidious and harder to account for when it comes to personal health. About two decades ago, the wired telephone was a luxury for society. Soon, to avoid the inconvenience of going to somebody's house to make a call, STD booths sprang up everywhere. Soon, walking to the STD booth became inconvenient and the fact that the conversation was not private added to this inconvenience. Then landlines became a common commodity but again, they came with their own share of inconveniences. Since landlines were wired, one had to go to the phone every time it rang, or one had to make a call. To resolve this inconvenience, wireless phones were introduced. Then to make the user experience more comfortable, the dial pad was replaced with a touch screen and today, one can simply ask Siri or Alexa to make a call. Also, earlier we also had to memorise numbers and navigate on our own but now there is no need to do this as well. How this change from STDs to smartphones has impacted the human mind and health is hard to say but there are numerous other examples that showcase this slow but steady takeover of convenience over humanity.

Today, using the body or mind in any form can be deemed inconvenient and using the latest innovation or gadget is more sought after even if it comes at a cost to our own health and environment. But what we fail to realise is that the desire for convenience is a serious threat to our health, and every human is addicted to it and suffers from it. This urge for convenience can be seen as a disease that has spread on a global level. We desire things to be done quickly and with less movement. We want to rest more and work less. We consume ready-to-eat and ready-to-drink products to save ourselves from cooking. In addition, we prefer a shortcut to weight loss through liposuction and weight-loss pills because regular exercise is inconvenient. Sleeping late is convenient and getting up early is inconvenient. In short, being disciplined and hard-working is inconvenient.

On the other hand, overlooking amenities that add convenience to our lives is also not a correct approach because it labels you as an orthodox if you continue to use old telephone sets and appliances. The truth is that change is inevitable, and it is beyond our control. Thus, we should be flexible to change but be mindful of our health as well. This is only possible if we regulate convenience in our lives and understand the benefits of inconvenience. Let's explore this in detail in the next section.

FIT Principle: Get Inconvenient

Though we all may find inconvenience truly inconvenient, it is an integral part of growth and progress and has an inherent quality that makes it beneficial for those who accept it. As mentioned earlier, the benefits of exercising are well-known, yet many find it inconvenient to exercise. The primary reason for this is that the mind intentionally discourages inconvenience of any sort and wants to avoid it. This is why laziness and procrastination have become the defining traits of humans. But this wasn't the case earlier. Our ancestors had a better and healthier lifestyle because they had to partake in more physical activity than the present generation. Options like televisions and computers were not available and so they did not have the choice to sit idle for a long time. A large part of the population worked in agriculture, which was laborious and intense physically. Also, children walked to their schools and adults cycled to their offices, and due to the lack of handy electrical kitchen appliances, women were much more physically active in daily household activities. Nevertheless, we can't definitively conclude that they were not sluggish and victimised by inconvenience.

In the last 20-30 years, with the advent of liberalisation, stiff industrialisation, and a paradigm shift in technology, the luxury of convenience has reached the masses due to which, the time spent on physical activity has reduced drastically. Lack of physical activity is the fourth leading cause of global mortality, causing an estimated 3.2 million deaths globally every year. It says that one in every three adults is inactive and has a 20-30 per cent higher risk of death than people who are active. Sitting, according to recent studies, is deadlier than smoking cigarettes. Research published in the Journal of the American College of Cardiology showed that women who sit for 10 or more hours a day might have a significantly greater risk of developing heart disease than those who sit for five hours or less. Sitting implies less physical movement, which reduces the blood flow, burns less fat, and clogs the heart with fat. It also slows down the digestion process and increases the risk of obesity, diabetes, cancer as well as depression. It can also lead to neck, hip, back, spine, and shoulder problems. Over time, inactivity leads to weak bones, which makes the body more prone to fractures. In a study, researchers looked at 47 studies examining the relationship between sitting and mortality and found that people who sit for long periods are 24 per cent more likely to die from health problems compared to people who sit less.

Depression and agility are linked inversely. That is, the more one stays active, and the less negativity surrounds the mind. So, how can we stay naturally active in contemporary settings? We will delve into this query in the next section.

Embrace Active Living

It is the law of nature that anything that is not used will lose its strength and become defunct with time. The same rule applies to the human body, and just like any other machine, it too needs regular movement to stay in good condition. Basically, when we engage in physical activities, our body becomes active and rejuvenated, and on the contrary, if we do not provide it with the necessary movement on a regular basis, it becomes weak. This is why it is essential to make a conscious effort to keep our bodies active and not give in to convenience.

One way we can achieve this is by designing our surroundings in a way that encourages movement. Keeping frequently used items at a distance from us means that we will have to get up and move to get them, which, in turn, will get our blood circulating and activate the muscles and metabolic systems as well. Devices, chargers, books, glasses, water bottles, remotes, and alarm clocks should always be at a distance so that when you need them, your body has to move back and forth to use them. Studies show that every time you get up and walk to pick up an object, the body burns 13 per cent more calories compared to just picking it up when it is lying next to you.

Another tip is to stack your everyday clothes on higher shelves in your wardrobe. This way, every time you reach with your hand for your clothes, you will enhance the blood flow to your artilleries and help decongest them, which will keep your heart healthy. Using the same application, you can store certain items in places which require you to bend. The reason being that every time you bend, your joints loosen up and your muscles have to use their strength to maintain that position against gravity. Moreover, every time you open the wardrobe, let your elbow be parallel to your heart while holding the door handles. This will strengthen your back muscles and help you keep cervical pains and frozen shoulders at bay. Also, use alternate hands to pick and hang your clothes.

Regular upward movement of the shoulders keeps the muscles and the rotator active. This is a contributing reason why women are less prone to cardiovascular diseases than men because they raise their hands above their shoulders often while doing household chores. Even the way women's clothing is designed involves moving their hands and shoulders above their heads in order to put it on or while taking it off. In high-rise flats and tiny balconies, it might be impractical but possible to find ways to hang your washed clothes higher to dry. Similarly, in the kitchen, keep the daily utensils on higher or extremely lower shelves, so you have to either stretch or sit in a squat position to get them. Squats build the right muscles to keep your foot's arch in shape. Try to eat while sitting cross-legged on the floor. Keep the refrigerator out of the kitchen so that you will have to walk back and forth, and deliberately invest time in being active, even while cooking. Let's look at some other activities that we can incorporate into our daily lives.

At home, try to open the door when it rings, rather than leaving the task to your house help or your children. Polish your shoes while kneeling down, lay the table for dinner, make the bed, take the pet for a walk, clean your car once in a while, play with your children, wipe your washroom floor after a bath, and cook a meal for your family on weekends. Try to walk short distances instead of taking your car.

Facilities such as online shopping and ordering though have added a lot of convenience to our lives, they have done so at the cost of our health. Every once in a while, try to walk to the grocery store or nearby market to buy what you want instead of ordering online. This way, your body will burn more calories and get more health benefits in the long run. Holding your grocery bags tight activates your shoulders. Use the same strategy for office files, documents, and stationery. Also, park the car at a distance so that the body can cover more space on foot. Walk down to your workstation more often, stand once every 15 minutes, walk to the farthest washroom in the office, and take the stairs instead of elevators. Remember that a sedentary lifestyle is the new smoking. Sitting for long hours inadvertently leads to poor posture and blood circulation, a weak digestive system, and an accumulation of fats. Invest in a standing desk or change your regular table into a standing one and alternate between standing and sitting.

By consciously taking control of our life and converting our daily routines into deliberate practices, we can achieve physical and mental fitness. Having an active lifestyle is way more beneficial for health than spending an hour at the gym. A recent study also revealed that an inactive lifestyle may completely negate the protective effects of a healthy set of genes. *Overall,* simply by being active, you improve your immune system, prevent joint pains, reduce your chances of getting the seasonal flu, balance your insulin levels, keep a check on your cholesterol, control your period flow, control stress, and keep your mind active.

Stretch Out to Health

In current times, pay more heed to things like strength, stamina, and weight but we fail to realise the importance of flexibility. And the key to building a flexible body is stretching. One of the major differences between the contemporary and our ancestor's lifestyles is that they stretched more often than we do in our daily routine today. Activities like moping the floor stretch the complete lower section of your body and also improve muscle strength in the legs. Also, the prevalence of Indian toilets required them to stretch their legs on a daily basis.

The important takeaway here is that stretching is the key when it comes to building a healthy body, joints, muscles, and bones. It also makes the body feel lighter and more active and also improves blood circulation, strengthens the muscles, and builds endurance. Given below are a few tips to keep in mind while you work on your stretches.

The muscles have to be warmed up before stretching, and you can know that they have been warmed up when the heart rate begins to increase. Each stretch has to be maintained for a minimum of 30 seconds, with a minimum of 20 minutes of stretching before and after a workout.

Yoga provides a great mix of stretching and breathing exercises that build a flexible and healthy body. For full body stretch, hanging on a bar without any movement stretches all your joints and muscles in one go.

* * *

So far, we have covered three fundamental principles of health, collectively known as the FIT principles. The 'F' signifies the importance of managing your emotions, 'T' stands for taking control of your dietary choices, and in this chapter, we have delved into the concept of cultivating an active lifestyle by embracing the principle of practising inconvenience. To achieve a state of optimal health, it's imperative to integrate all three principles into your daily routine. The absence of any one of these principles in your routine puts your health at risk. Therefore, incorporating the FIT principles as the cornerstone of your daily health philosophy is crucial, offering a straightforward formula for achieving gratifying health outcomes. Moreover, in the forthcoming chapters, we will cover some more principles that will further enhance your journey towards well-being.

Chapter XI

The Best Doctor

'Every prescription can't be written.'

One of the initial impetuses for me to explore the subject of health was an incident with a doctor. I took my daughter to this doctor as she was feeling unwell. He simply held my daughter's hand and prescribed a treatment, which left me curious about the fact that whether, in some cases, diagnosing and monitoring health could be so simple that it doesn't require the intervention of experts or complicated procedures. This book and particularly this chapter are the outcome of this experience and I have tried my best to research and compile relevant information pertaining to this topic. It may not be complete, but it is sure to provide you with insights that will allow you to monitor your health and take ownership of it and avoid the need for frequent medical interventions. With these practical tips, you can start living a healthier and more fulfilling life.

***

Over the years, the medical industry has seen exponential growth primarily because of the high demand for medical services. And this demand doesn't seem to be decreasing anytime soon and instead is constantly increasing. On top of that, understanding and navigating through this new medical system has become extremely difficult due to its complex nature. Nowadays, you can find specialised doctors for each and every body part and system. And this specialisation requires years of training and in-depth knowledge which makes us feel incapable of taking charge of our own health and increases our reliance on these institutions, which, in turn, further boosts the medical industry.

But the important point to realise here is the myth that health is too complicated a subject which needs to be left to the experts. The truth is that our health lies in our own hands and thus, we have a bigger role to play when it comes to our personal health. This doesn't mean that we need to completely forgo medical sciences; instead, it means that medical sciences usually come into the picture once a health issue has arisen that needs an expert's assistance. But we can play a crucial role by being more cognisant of the symptoms and to what diseases it is pointing to and then nipping the issue in the bud. And to do so, we need to be aware of the signs that our body is giving us and what these signs mean. Therefore, we need to pay attention to minor discomforts, pain, fever, cough, vomiting, anxiety, or any uneasy signs that show that something is hindering our health.

Also, these signs are actually not the main issue or disease but early symptoms of the upcoming disease. For example, we might think that indigestion is a problem, but it could be hinting towards the fact that we are not chewing our food properly or wearing tight clothing. Thus, it is important to be cognisant of the sign that our body is showing and the issue behind it. And by becoming more adept at listening to signals of our body, we will be able to better manage our health and also avoid several unnecessary hassles. The truth is that the significance of a quick diagnosis and quick action cannot be overstated.

So, let us study some of the signs that we need to be mindful of and what they mean.

- **Bowel Movement and Faeces**

  The GI tract (gastrointestinal tract) enables a smooth processing of food from the time it enters the mouth till it excretes from the body through the anus. And by testing our excretion process and faeces daily, we can deduce the efficiency of the digestion and the nutrient absorption process from the food. This, in turn, will give us a good picture of our overall health.

  Studies have shown us that the defecation time ranging from a few seconds to a few minutes is fine. But if it takes an extraordinarily long time or you have to push hard to clear your bowels or you pass gas while doing so, it is time to review your last day's diet and routine. And if this happens often or on a regular basis, then it is important to review your eating habits and whole eating process. At times, even when you are eating right, there could be other factors affecting your bowel movement such as not chewing properly, less fibrous or high protein food, low water consumption, unsystematic meal timings, style of cooking, eating with an open mouth, drinking water while eating, etc.

Apart from our bowel movement, our excrement can also give us an accurate measure of general health. The parameters that we need to consider are the texture and the colour of the waste. Normally, a hard or semi-solid texture passed out with a little intermittent gas and enforcing pressure to release is a sign of a more acidic diet or semi-digested food due to any of the reasons stated above. Surprisingly, water makes up two-thirds of the healthiest bowel movement, and the rest is a combination of dead and alive cells, mucus, and fibre. A very regular hard stool implies a high carbohydrate or protein diet coupled with a lack of fluids or fibre.

On the shade card, a healthy colour of excrement is considered to be golden yellow with a smooth semi-solid form and at times, the colours green and brown are fine too. The green colour indicates that green leafy vegetables have passed through the intestine without bile addition. On the other hand, the spots of red or black mean the presence of liquid or dried blood which might be due to some infection or pain in the gut or could also be an early symptom of the piles. Both scenarios require consultation and a change in daily routine and diet. If the faeces are of any other colour, then it requires regular monitoring and if it doesn't get better with a change in eating habits, then consult a doctor. Floating faeces indicate a more acidic and fatty diet while the more alkaline and balanced your diet is, the better your faeces will sink.

Another aspect which is generally not well-known is the aspect of how we poop. Back in the day, our ancestors would do the deed in designated spots as the facility of toilets wasn't available. Later, the ground toilet (also known as the Indian toilet) emerged which was designed in such a way that it required the person to go into a squatting posture in order to excrete. This squatting posture, in which the knees touch the chest and thighs, and the spine is at an angle of almost 35 degrees, is the best and most natural posture for effortless bowel movement. If you do not want to go to the toilet more than once a day, then excreting in a squatting posture is the best way to clean the bowel in one go. But nowadays, even in developing countries, the squatting toilet has been replaced by the English toilet. This again harkens back to the inconvenient principle. The English toilet is an example of convenience because we found it inconvenient to sit in a squatting posture. And so, we desired to sit comfortably on a seat while excretion, but this convenience came at a cost—improper bowel movement which in turn led to issues such as constipation, haemorrhoids, and colon cancer. In today's modern world, most of us are using English toilets due to their ubiquitousness. And even if want to use the Indian-style toilet, it would not only require a big lifestyle change but also an infrastructural change. But there is an easy alternative. You can simply convert the English toilet into an Indian toilet by placing a stool under your feet. The level of the stool should be such that your thighs should touch your stomach and your knees should touch or be close to your chest. This way you can avail all the benefits of an Indian toilet through your English toilet. Just make sure that your feet are not parallel to your butt but slightly outside. Also, ensure that the main body weight is on your feet, and you should be gently resting on the seat. These specially designed toilet stools are available on most e-commerce websites.

- **Farts**

  Not many people know this but farts are good indicators of our health. It is fine to release gas as long as it does not stink. Habits like open-mouth eating, talking while eating, and eating after long gaps lead to inhalation of air that passes through the GI tract and comes out as a fart with or without a sound. Another reason for farts could be an incomplete bowel cleansing which leads the faeces to decay and become acidic. Generally, half-chewed or half-cooked food delays digestion and ferments in the stomach and the longer it stays, the more acidic it becomes and generates gas. The most acidic foods like beans, nuts, and eggs react with stomach acids and generate gas. On this basis, a well-chewed rich meal taken on time keeps the fart away.

- **Urine**

  Similar to faeces and farts, our urine too can reveal a lot about our health. Normally, the urine is pale in colour, and it is not only a sign of good health but also an indication of good water intake. Dark yellow urine indicates dehydration due to less fluid consumption or can also be due to certain medicines. However, urine should not have a strong smell. With dehydration or a UTI infection, the urine becomes more concentrated and may give out a stronger ammonia scent than normal and on the other hand, the sweet odour is a sign of uncontrolled or pre-diabetes. Colours like pink or red may be due to some coloured vegetables; otherwise, it is a serious disorder and could be due to a kidney infection, UTI, or prostate tumour.

  High frequency of urination is not a problem, since with age, the relevant muscles in the body get weak and lose the strength to hold urine for a longer period. For people who have sex regularly, the muscles remain strong enough to hold urine for longer periods and to throw urine away from the body while urination. Regular urination with low throw pressure is a sign of low energy and fatigue which can be due to vitamin or mineral deficiencies and must be treated. Also, a constant change in urine colour, if not due to any medication, requires a consultation as well.

- **Sleep**

The importance of sleep cannot be overstated. Even an active life and a good diet cannot guarantee good health without a proper sleep cycle. Let's look at some aspects that show the importance of sleep.

Body fat burns approximately fourteen hours after exercising, especially between 11 p.m. and early morning, when the body is in deep sleep. On the other hand, if you are not sleeping properly and feel tired and fatigued most of the day, the exercise will not be effective. This is also the reason why the body weight always varies before and after sleep because the body loses weight during sleep and without proper rest, weight loss will not be effective. Remember that 84 per cent of weight loss occurs through the nose, and the same rule applies while sleeping. Likewise, the process through which nutrients are supplied to every cell in our body and toxins are released cannot be performed by the brain while it is awake. Therefore, when the body sleeps, the brain acts as a housekeeper, making it ready for active processing and compromising on sleep can lead to an increase in anxiety, anger, stress, and irritation in the brain.

On the other hand, good sleep enhances concentration, improves decision-making skills, activates social skills and boosts creativity. Basically, sleep is like hitting the refresh button for the brain as well as the entire body. Eight hours is the average sleep required by individuals of all ages. For young children, the requirement is more than that and it reduces with age. Sleeping straight on the back is healthy for growing children as it helps the body to relax.

Sleep deprivation may not have an immediate impact on our health but will do so at later stages of life. As Tim Bitchen said, 'Sleep is god. Go worship it.' A sleep-deprived brain cannot even form memories. A study conducted on mice showed that the human brain needs sleep to refresh it and that it can store information only up to a certain capacity which is restored during sleep.

It is a proven fact that less than seven hours of sleep makes the body three times more prone to catching a cold than a normal person. During sleep, the detoxification process removes toxins from the body, and our acid levels are highest between one and three o'clock in the early hours. If the body has ingested high quantities of acidic food, it will face more disturbed periods of sleep around these hours. With an alkaline-rich dinner, the body's metabolism works smoothly which in turn prevents any disturbance during deep sleep hours. Changing positions quite often at night is a sign of heavy and acidic eating habits.

In recent times, our sleep quality has taken a tremendous hit due to screen time and other distractions. Good sleep requires a conducive environment. Thus, it is important to keep your lights dim and devices out of reach while sleeping. Lie down in your bed, set the room temperature to your comfort, read a book, breathe deeply, and wear comfortable sleeping clothes.

- **Nails**

  Nails can indicate several deficiencies and health problems. White spots are signs of fungal infection, while horizontal white lines are early signs of diabetes, circulatory diseases, or recent severe illnesses. Cracked nails are symptoms of thyroid or prostate problems due to low immunity. Protein or nutritional deficiencies make the nails brittle and fragile. However, this can sometimes also be a result of chemicals used during a manicure or pedicure. Black lines, if not due to a blood clot under the nail or some injury, signal a serious skin disorder, cancer, or cardiovascular disease.

- **Teeth**

  A dry mouth can be an indicator of various dental disorders such as tooth decay, discolouration of teeth and gums, and bad breath. These conditions are among the most frequently occurring dental ailments. Dry mouth can be caused by mouth-breathing, dehydration, or medications used to treat high blood pressure, anxiety, and overactive bladder. Drinking water regularly in small amounts can help keep the mouth hydrated. Maintaining good oral hygiene, reducing alcohol consumption, and avoiding chewing gum can also keep the salivary glands active. Certain natural remedies such as rubbing cayenne pepper, fennel seeds, cardamom, and ginger on the tongue may also help. Consuming low-acidic foods can alleviate dry mouth as well.

- **Pulse**

Pulse checking is an age-old method used to quickly assess an individual's health status. It remains standard practice today and is often the first thing a doctor will check during a medical examination.

The normal pulse rate among male adults is anything between 65-75, 70-80 for females, and 80-90 for children while newborns may have a pulse rate as high as 140. Anything above 85-90 indicates a weak heart and a high chance of heart strokes or related diseases. A high heart rate coupled with high blood pressure and cholesterol can help identify potential health problems.

Checking your pulse on a weekly basis is a healthy habit. The ideal time to check your pulse rate is when your body is at rest, i.e., your RHR or

Resting Heart Rate. Your pulse rate after exercise, alcohol, sex, coffee, or even while the body is stressed may not be your regular RHR. The pulse can be measured at the wrist, just below the thumb, or on both sides of the neck; some experts can even check it on the tip of your feet or at the elbow.

- **Other Signs**

  Many conditions like sprains, strains, injuries, and infections can cause swelling. Tight shoes may swell the feet, especially in the case of a sedentary lifestyle. This may also occur due to low circulation of blood and retention of fluids in some parts of the body due to pregnancy, obesity, or certain medications. Regular retention of fluids in the feet, ankles, or legs could be a sign of the heart pumping less blood. Being more active, moving regularly, and standing quite often in between sedentary work can improve blood circulation and reduce swelling. Widespread swelling is a serious cause of concern and can be a serious symptom of kidney or heart failure, allergic reactions, venomous bites, or diseases like diabetes. It needs a physician's consultation immediately.

  Although dry skin during winter or after a hot water shower is common, consistently getting dry skin could be an indication of dehydration, thyroid, diabetes, and even heart-related diseases. Thyroid and diabetes leach moisture from the skin due to the deficiency of nutrients from acidic diets. Dryness or patchy skin on the legs, shins, or feet may be due to oxygen-deprived skin which can cause narrowing of the heart arteries. Other than dryness, dark skin patches are also signs of diabetes, extra fat, or even in rare cases, cancer. Also, early signs of wrinkles can imply low bone density or osteoporosis. Pimples or ulcers on the face or mouth, which are accompanied by slight pain, can be caused by a variety of factors, including high temperatures in the body as well as highly acidic food. Also, rashes might occur due to allergies or medicines, but if they last more than three days, they require consultation.

Eyes can also reveal a lot about internal health. Yellow eyes indicate liver disorders and high cholesterol. It can also mean that the ducts that carry the bile away from the liver are blocked. Dry eyes are the side effects of high screen time or medications like sleeping pills, anxiety, or pain relievers. Itchy, swollen, and red eyes may be caused by allergies due to dust, pollen, or pet dander.

Feeling less energetic, constantly fatigued, and not being able to focus are the indications to be mindful of. Revisit your sleep pattern and self-assess whether you are getting enough sleep. Apart from sleep, dietary habits can also make the body lethargic. Excessive sugar and processed foods can also imbalance the energy distribution of the body. Apart from this, dehydration, medication, stress, and anxiety can also make the body feel tired and moody. But if the reason for tiredness is none of the above, it is advisable to consult a doctor and get your deficiencies tested.

The point to note here is that neither did Mother Nature design any diet charts, nor did she construct any hospitals in jungles. All she did was create an ecosystem of flora and fauna around us and instilled in us with intellect to sustain health from them and draw conclusions for ourselves. And though we required hospitals in cases of emergencies and accidents, we also let them flourish by being ignorant of core health principles. First, we exploited ourselves with unhealthy lifestyles and then surrendered our bodies to these specialists and doctors to experiment with medicines, surgeries, and studies at the cost of our health and lives. The increasing number of hospitals indicates a lack of self-care and the failure to practice the evergreen principles compiled in this book. The fact remains that there is no better doctor for you than yourself. There is no better spiritual guide for you than yourself. All in all, the more self-aware we become, the less we need to consult doctors.

Chapter XII

The Best Relation

'To keep a relationship healthy, you will need to do something new every day. And this includes your relationship with others as well as with yourself.'

If the main goal of maintaining good health is to increase lifespan, then individuals who have lived long can attest that healthy relationships are the key to a healthy and happy life. In this session, we will explore the life cycle of a relationship, the importance of being socially engaged, and a simple matrix to identify healthy relationships that directly contribute to a holistic life.

***

The pursuit of happiness is a fundamental goal in life for everyone. But what truly makes us happy? A long-term study conducted by Harvard University involving 724 individuals from diverse backgrounds and cultures aimed to answer this question. The study, which went on for 75 years, closely followed the lives, families, health, professions, eating habits, and social lives of the participants and recorded and analysed their statements, observations, and views. The researchers found that the individuals who lived a long, happy, and healthy life also had healthy relationships. Family bonds, trust in friends and relatives, and respect for strangers are all important factors that contribute to a peaceful and healthy life. However, the current trend of using technology as a medium of conversation is changing the way we approach relationships. Conversations have shifted to chats and emotions are being expressed through likes and forwards. Due to this paradigm shift in how we interact with people has made it difficult to maintain true bonds. And if we want to know what really works in a relationship to keep it afresh, happy, and healthy, we can do so by understanding the lifecycle of a relationship.

The Age of Relationship and Its Significance

In today's world, staying connected with family and friends has become easier than ever before through social media. We have access to their whereabouts, vacation updates, family developments, and the latest happenings, making it easy to stay up to date with their lives. However, just staying connected is not enough to ensure healthy relationships.

To maintain a strong connection, we need to continually work on the relationships we share with various people. However, it's equally important to recognise the signs of an unhealthy relationship and address them before they escalate. Couples may trust each other, communicate well, and share household responsibilities, but it's crucial to assess whether they are genuinely happy in their relationship. Let's look at an example that shows how a relationship begins and matures.

A relationship typically begins with a spark. This might be a moment of eye contact or small talk that turns into longer conversations, and with this sense of joy and excitement, a new relationship begins. This is the infancy stage of the relationship. Gradually, the couple makes a commitment to be in an official relationship. During this baby stage, the relationship is brimming with all kinds of expressions of love and romance blossoms in full swing. Soon a kid enters into this relationship and your love is distributed between your significant other and the baby. This is when your relationship enters the 'adult age'. Next, the kids grow up and so do your responsibilities, which include your child's education, finances, career, health, marriage, etc. Then your kids have children of their own and they take over your attention, and this way, your love further divides, but it is not weakened in any way. But by this time, the age of the relationship has reached its last stage. All this while, life was pretty good with its ups and downs, but an important question still remains unanswered—Are you happy? The only reason for this pause is that during all the stages of the relationship, love existed, but what was missing all along was the expression of love.

When we were in our infancy, we prioritised expressing our love. We gave pleasant surprises, found reasons to celebrate every small occasion, and made sure every moment of togetherness was filled with love and appreciation. The love just grew, and the expression of love at this stage just made everything about the relationship so fulfilling and happy. However, the mistake begins at the adult age, when we stop expressing our love, and this carries on until the love turns old. This means that having love for someone is not enough; we have to find ways to express it.

One of the primary issues that negatively impact all kinds of relationships is the fact that we often withhold our love and appreciation for the other person and do not express it wholly. It also might be the case that love exists in the relationship but what is missing is the expression of love. And this leads to an incomplete relationship which, in turn, leaves a vacuum within us. Simply put, we love but do not express it. We care but do not mention it. We miss people but hold our words. We like things about people but do not compliment them. We remember the good times but do not discuss them.

Thus, in order to evaluate a relationship, we need to assess whether we express our love to our loved ones, children, friends, relatives, peers, parents and everyone we love and care about. And the day the expression of love is lost, the happiness in the relationship begins to vanish. Apart from expressing love through words, you should also incorporate actions and habits that show your love like remembering anniversaries, giving a hug to all your family members every day, etc. One of the simple ways we can build strong relationships is by talking about something new other than mundane and compulsive conversations. This helps in keeping happiness alive in your relationships. So, tell your parents that you love them. Meet your friends, listen to them, and show your interest in what is happening in their lives. Dale Carnegie says, 'You can make more friends in two days by being interested in other people than you can in two years by trying to get other people interested in you.'

Types of Relations

Relationships heal; they work as medicine. A healthy relationship can be as good as healthy food or a good day in a gym. But which are those relations that make us feel healthy? It is vital to understand them in order to navigate and nurture our connections with others, whether they be personal, professional, or societal. We can understand them through the relation matrix given below. In your day-to-day life, all the people you meet, either you know them, or you do not know them. The people you know include those with whom you stay, work, study, travel, etc. The people you don't know are the ones with whom you rarely interact and usually exchange general greetings and well wishes.

	People You Know	People You Don't Know
Conditional Relations	**Relatives** People with whom we have a connection but have limited heartfelt communication	**Acquaintances** People with whom we have occasional interaction/communication
Unconditional Relations	**Close Friends and Family** People with whom we have a close and sincere connection	**Idols and Icons** People we look up to and are influenced by

I. Conditional Relations

Conditional relations involve actions driven by specific motives or expectations of reciprocity. Individuals within these relationships are often unaware of each other's weaknesses, interests, likes, dislikes, etc. These relationships are governed by conditions; if you treat them well, they will reciprocate in kind.

- **Relatives**

  This is a conditional category that consists of people you share a direct connection with, like relatives such as your cousins, uncles, aunts, in-laws, etc., but you may or may not share a close relationship with them. You typically encounter them during specific events and gatherings, and if your interactions are limited to these occasions and don't extend beyond them, these can be classified as conditional relationships.

- **Acquaintances**

  This category consists of people whom you speak to or meet often in your day-to-day life and though you know who they are, you lack a connection with them on a deeper level. This could be due to the fact that your interactions with them only concern professional or related matters or because you interact with them only through social media. Some of the people who fall into this category are your neighbours, colleagues, peers, subordinates, school friends, teachers, travellers, and distant relatives. Most relationships other than your family fall into this category, and the moment you begin to express your love, the infancy stage begins. These relationships are neutral to health.

II. Unconditional Relations

Unconditional relations involve selflessly giving without expecting anything in return. The people who fall into this category accept the way you are.

- **Close Family and Friends**

  These are the people you know in and out, and you can express your heart to them without any reservation. This includes your love, spouse, mother, father, sister, brother, child, friends, etc. People within this group are dependable and their presence makes you feel secure and brings happiness to you. These relations, whether romantic, familial, or platonic, play a profound role in shaping your well-being and overall quality of life and increasing your healthy lifespan.

- **Idols and Icons**

  This group consists of people whom you know, but they don't know you or may not know much about you. This can be an actor, artist, leader, spiritual leader, teacher, or any ordinary person who you believe in or admire. An important aspect of this lot of people is that even though your relationship with them may be very limited, they play an extremely important role in your life.

This relationship matrix is very dynamic, and one has to keep adding, deleting, or shuffling people as they evolve within the relationship cycle. But it is critical to identify the most nutritious relationship and nurture them. If you find yourself with few or no connections to list in the friends and family category, it's likely that you are experiencing a sense of isolation and living a socially unhealthy life. The straightforward path to cultivating social well-being is by connecting with others and expressing yourself.

Numerous studies have demonstrated the profound impact of positive relationships on our mental and physical health. Emotionally supportive connections reduce stress levels, increase self-esteem, reduce the risk of developing chronic diseases, help in recovering more quickly from illnesses, and provide us with a sense of belonging and security. The prescription to get all these healthy benefits is by simply expressing yourself through words, touch, gestures, care, and love.

Chapter XIII

The Best Trait

'The ultimate purpose behind every action, gesture, or thought is happiness.'

Health is not just about dieting and exercising; your nature and habits define your longevity too. Imagine waking up every morning feeling energised, motivated, and ready to tackle whatever challenges come your way. The impact of cultivating healthy habits and personal traits cannot be quantified, and anything that makes you feel good and helps you express your emotions can be as beneficial as meditation or proper nourishment. One must discover what brings them a sense of well-being and incorporate those things into their character as traits. In this chapter, we will delve into some universally beneficial traits and examine how they can be cultivated for a healthier, happier you.

- **A Date with Nature**

  Nature is a natural healer, and being around it can be therapeutic for our minds and bodies. It can increase energy levels, reduce stress hormones and depression, and build immunity. Unfortunately, our modern lifestyles often leave little time for us to connect with nature. Most of us spend time indoors and hardly get any exposure to sunlight, fresh air, or greenery. Research has shown that living in green areas can improve mental health, concentration, and memory and foster positive relationships. There are still options to find green spaces in urban areas, and we should take advantage of them. On the other side, living in enclosed environments with artificial surroundings can have adverse effects on our health. Poorly ventilated homes can lead to respiratory problems, infections, and seasonal flu.

- **The Power of Giving**

Positivity is a quality that emanates from within and is unlocked through kindness. It's a fundamental trait expected of every human being by Mother Nature, and one that everyone should strive to embody. Practising kindness towards oneself and the environment is not only essential but also a responsibility, especially for those blessed with wealth and resources. When money, knowledge, skills, and wealth are in the hands of individuals who understand the importance of kindness, their investments and utilisation tend to be more meaningful and wiser.

Giving, however, isn't limited to material possessions alone. One can give in various ways, such as volunteering time, supporting meaningful causes, or sharing knowledge. Contributing to religious institutions, NGOs, and charitable trusts that tirelessly work towards noble causes is a powerful avenue for spreading kindness. The act of giving is not only fulfilling but also possesses the remarkable ability to heal and nurture, often returning to the giver in abundance.

Kindness finds expression in numerous forms, even for those who may not have financial resources to spare. It can be as simple as refraining from bargaining over petty amounts when dealing with hardworking individuals, assisting elderly or handicapped beggars, delivering water to the less fortunate during scorching summers, offering your time to teach underprivileged children, or supporting impoverished street vendors. Acts like these not only bring a smile to the faces of those you help but also contribute to your own well-being.

- **Clean Living**

When it comes to health, cleanliness encompasses the aspect of a clean heart, body, and mind. A clean heart entails releasing any burdens that generate negativity. It's crucial to have a support system in which you can confide your thoughts and emotions with trusted friends and family. While it's not necessary to share everything with the same person, bottling up your feelings and problems can result in underlying disturbances.

Maintaining bodily cleanliness extends beyond basic hygiene practices such as handwashing and daily showers. It also encompasses the upkeep of cleanliness in your surroundings and home, wearing clean clothes, which, in turn, aids in decluttering your mind and averting negative emotions. Being mindful of unclean environments and things, such as ATMs, mobile phones, and public transportation, is vital as they can expose you to harmful bacteria and contagious diseases. Neglecting these factors can lead to severe health issues.

- **The Power of Intimacy**

Did you know that a simple kiss can burn up to 26 calories? That's just the beginning of the benefits that come with being intimate. From the expression of love to the act of sexual intercourse, the body is activated in a way that is satisfying on both emotional and physical levels. The chemicals that are released during intimacy, such as oxytocin and endorphins, generate feelings of happiness and pleasure. But there are many other benefits that go beyond just emotional satisfaction.

Intimacy can increase oxygen flow and improve your heartbeat rate, which is great for your cardiovascular health. It exercises your muscles, releases stress, and even burns fat in the right places. It can also do wonders for your skin and hair, leaving you looking and feeling younger and more vibrant.

But the health benefits of intimacy go beyond just physical appearance. Regular intimacy can reduce the risk of prostate cancer in men and lower the risk of urinary tract infections in both men and women. It can also help strengthen the muscles of the pelvic floor, which can reduce the risk of incontinence later in life.

So, don't just think of intimacy as a way to feel good. Think of it as a way to improve your overall health and well-being. Whether it's through kissing, holding hands, or sexual intercourse, being active in your intimacy can do wonders for your mind and body.

- **Admiring Self-Appearance**

The desire to look good is a form of self-care and wellness therapy that we can apply to ourselves. In our society, we often find ourselves judging others while also being acutely aware of the impressions we make on those around us. This behaviour stems from a natural human inclination to seek approval and compliments, as they boost confidence and provide a subtle, hidden sense of happiness.

The emphasis on looking good has likely existed since the dawn of humanity, driven by the innate attraction to beauty, especially when it comes to attracting potential partners. To experience this wonderful feeling, one must consistently invest in themselves. This includes maintaining a healthy, flexible, and well-shaped body through disciplined fitness routines, enjoying visits to beauty salons, styling one's hair, undergoing makeovers, indulging in spa treatments, and ensuring personal hygiene.

Regardless of age or circumstances, it's always possible to make an effort to present oneself in an up-to-date and appealing manner. Wearing ill-fitting or excessively tight clothing not only looks awkward but can also lead to digestive issues, nerve disorders, and even joint pain. On the other hand, dressing in loose or well-fitted attire during the workweek and opting for comfortable, body-friendly textiles during weekends at home is a healthy approach to fashion.

Cultivating a desire to look good and taking pride in your appearance can lead to greater self-discipline in adhering to health and wellness principles. The more you see yourself in the mirror, the more motivated and conscious you become about maintaining a healthy and attractive appearance.

- **Sports**

Sports are not just about physical exercise; it's also about the emotional release that comes with playing a game. How many professions in the world offer you the chance to openly display your joy and sense of accomplishment in front of others? How often have you met your sales targets and celebrated by running through office halls or in the streets? Yet, a simple game of sports, even on your neighbourhood street, offers that opportunity with every wicket, every goal, every smash, every stroke, or at every point scored.

Human beings have a natural inclination for play and the resulting joy it brings. Whether it's an indoor or outdoor game, engaging in sports fosters connections and serves as an enjoyable stress-relieving activity.

- **Listening/Learning Music**

  Singing and listening to music evoke feelings of happiness. Engaging in musical activities, whether it's playing an instrument or singing, brings enlightenment and diverts your mind from physical stress. Have you ever wondered why we tend to exercise more effectively when there is music playing? It is because music captivates the mind, diverting it from the body's physical responses. Activities like singing in the shower, participating in karaoke sessions, and listening to the melodies of birds, the soothing sounds of streams, the rhythmic tides of oceans, or the peaceful ambience of a dense forest have a calming effect on our well-being.

- **Reading**

  Books have a healing quality. Reading can be likened to meditation because it necessitates the concentration of your conscious mind, fostering positive thoughts and inner peace while relieving stress. It keeps the brain active, bolsters concentration, and can even slow the progression of, or prevent, conditions like Alzheimer's and dementia. Furthermore, reading fuels creativity, often leading to the emergence of some of life's most brilliant ideas. Engaging in reading before tackling an important assignment or demanding task helps sharpen your focus and soothes your mind, making you more adept at problem-solving. The more you read, the better you become at expressing yourself.

To cultivate a reading habit, consider creating a dedicated reading corner in your home adorned with decorative shelves to prominently display your book collection. This constant visual reminder will inspire you to read more. Maintain a diverse collection of books, including short stories, motivational quotes, comics, reference materials, and poetry books, near your toilet seat for easy access during leisure moments. Lastly, make it a habit to carry a book with you while travelling to seize any opportunity to read and expand your knowledge.

- **Be Hopeful**

Without dreams, there would be no achievements. It is a healthy practice to frequently visit the realm of future success in your mind and envision fairy tales, effectively experiencing success beforehand. Dreams have the power to ignite your creativity, infuse passion into your endeavours, inspire you to lead a purposeful life, and take charge of your destiny. Maintaining hope is not only beneficial but also the driving force that propels us forward, preventing us from giving up. Dreams give rise to ideas that can lead you to discover your true calling. They often begin as a single persistent thought and, with dedication, can transform into multi-billion-dollar enterprises.

To realise your dreams, it's essential to take gradual steps to move forward, acquire relevant knowledge, cultivate relationships with like-minded individuals, engage in studies and attain certifications, and identify someone you wish to inspire, as they will fuel your passion. Even the smallest daily stride toward your dream constitutes success. Remember, failures serve as valuable lessons that belong to the past. Dreams are a lifelong source of joy, so make them a part of your daily to-do list and let them flourish.

* * *

This book is coming to a close, but the journey to health persists. And while certain universal qualities bring pleasure, there are countless unique experiences that contribute to health and happiness. The book's purpose is not to impose compulsive principles but to encourage readers to develop their own principles and traits that foster healthy living. *Healthy, Ever After* is a tribute to Mother Nature's most entrusted caretaker, and the story of SMILE will reveal who that caretaker is.

Chapter XIV

THE STORY OF SMILE

'It is only genes that are carried forward generation after generation. Everything else is short-lived.'

—Sudha Murthy

After a long day of toiling in the fields, an elderly peasant returned home. His youngest daughter, Shatarupa, kindly offered him a glass of water before disappearing into the kitchen. A little while later, she noticed her father wearing a self-assured smile.

Intrigued, Shatarupa approached her father and inquired, 'Baba, why do you have such a contented smile on your face?'

The peasant chuckled and replied, 'Smiles, my dear, that's my profession.'

Amused, Shatarupa asked, 'How can one make a living from smiling, Baba?'

'It's quite simple,' he explained. 'You just share it.'

As they both shared a laugh, Baba invited Shatarupa to sit down and listen as he elaborated on the philosophy behind his 'smile business'. He recounted a question his friend had once posed: 'Who is the most important person in your life?' Initially, Baba's response included his parents and himself, but his friend encouraged him to consider the concept of self-care.

He continued, 'By fulfilling our basic needs, such as eating, drinking, and working, we ensure our well-being. And in meeting these needs, we also assist others in fulfilling their own. In this way, we are all interconnected, supporting one another.' Shatarupa understood that it was all about cooperation, spreading smiles, and nurturing well-being.

She asked why smiles, specifically, and Baba explained that a smile transcends language and culture, symbolising happiness, respect, gratitude, and love. Baba's friend believed that the word 'SMILE' embodied health, with each letter representing a fundamental aspect of well-being. The elderly peasant then delved into the profound wisdom he had accumulated over the years, revealing the depth of the smile's significance in promoting a joyful and healthy life. Each letter of 'SMILE' corresponds to an element of educating about healthy living, which must be passed on to others to continue the chain of promoting well-being.

- **Sunshine**

  The Earth relies heavily on solar energy for its survival, and the same goes for humans. We thrive under the nourishing rays of the sun, which rejuvenate our bodies, elevate our spirits, and connect us to the radiant energy required to lead a meaningful life. While it's commonly believed that sunshine helps our bodies produce vitamin D, the truth is that every cell in the human body is directly or indirectly powered by the sun. Without the sun, there would be no plant life on Earth, and consequently, no source of energy for the planet's inhabitants to thrive. Every nutrient necessary for the human body and mind, every calorie we burn, is sourced from the sun's energy within our cells.

If you find yourself spending minimal time in the sun, there is a possibility that you are not leading the happiest and healthiest lifestyle possible. When sunlight hits our retinas, our bodies stimulate the production of serotonin, a chemical that plays a crucial role in uplifting our moods. Although it can be challenging to get adequate sun exposure in our busy lives, making it a practice to first gaze at the sun for a few moments when you step outside and avoiding sunglasses can be an effective way to start your day on a happier and healthier note. To tap into its power, bask in the sun whenever you can.

- **Everything in Moderation**

If I was asked to define health in a single word, I would say, moderation. Balance is the key to a healthy and happy life! It's a simple approach that involves maintaining an equilibrium and not overdoing anything, whether it's eating, exercising, or even thinking. The truth is that the extreme of anything is not good, no matter how healthy it may seem. Even eating too many green vegetables or being too attached to the idea of living healthily can be harmful. That's why moderation is the key to a balanced and healthy life.

One thing that moderation teaches is that nothing in life is black or white and everything can be done in moderation. This is why you can find extremely healthy people indulging in and enjoying all kinds of diets and lifestyles. This is possible because they do so in moderation. Remember that even venom can have medicinal value if used in moderation.

So, don't be afraid to indulge in your favourite foods or activities from time to time. Just remember to do so in moderation and find balance in everything you do. By following this simple approach, you can enjoy a healthy and happy life for years to come!

- **Refine Your Interest**

  Principles of health are universal, but our journey towards health is unique for all. The truth is that our perspectives, views, knowledge, beliefs, actions, and most importantly, our interests, define us as an individual. In fact, no teacher, doctor, parent, or friend can force you to do something you don't want to do. The choices stem only from our personal interests. Books, articles, inspiring stories, advice, and guidance will come and go, but our interest governs if they stay with us and for how long. For example, a coach or a teacher will teach the same technique to everyone, but only a few become Sachin Tendulkar or MS Dhoni or Shahrukh Khan or Mahatma Gandhi

The amount of attention an individual gives their health can be gleaned from their physical and mental health. Succinctly put, your attitude, behaviour, knowledge and skill set are the product of your interest. It governs the choices you make and decides your point of view on all aspects of life.

- **Legs and Lungs**

  Robust leg muscles and healthy lungs have a symbiotic relationship that represents a healthy physical trait. During physical exertion, when the leg muscles begin to tire, the lungs come into play, enhancing endurance to keep you going. Conversely, strong lungs play a vital role in aiding the legs to perform optimally, facilitating proper muscle development and coordination. When both the legs and lungs are robust and well-conditioned, your body is primed for activity.

  Maintaining a focus on the health of both your legs and lungs should be an integral part of your commitment to a healthy lifestyle. This dual approach not only aids in burning more calories but also contributes to overall well-being. Healthy lungs support the proper functioning of vital organs, including the digestive and respiratory systems, help regulate blood pressure, and enhance overall fitness.

> To ensure the vitality of both your legs and lungs, you can turn to timeless practices rooted in natural principles. These practices include attention to foot arch management, the adoption of correct breathing techniques, mindfulness of your breath, and participation in activities such as sprinting and squatting. Embracing these natural approaches fosters a harmonious balance between physical fitness and respiratory health, ultimately leading to a more active and rewarding life.

'It's quite intriguing,' Shatarupa remarked. 'You've shared the story of SMILE with me, but you haven't mentioned your friend's name yet.'

Baba responded with another warm smile. 'I had a feeling you'd find it captivating and would ask about my friend. In fact, it was my friend who suggested that I share this story with you one day.'

'Thank you,' Shatarupa expressed her gratitude. 'I intend to share this story as well. Everyone should be aware of it for the sake of their health and overall well-being.'

'Tell me, Baba,' Shatarupa inquired, 'who is your friend? Who shared this story with you?'

Baba gazed into her eyes and smiled affectionately. 'The friend who told me this story is your mother.'

According to her, women play a vital role in nurturing their families' well-being, happiness, and values. They are the guardians of good health. Baba emphasised the importance of mothers passing on their knowledge about health to their daughters, along with this heartwarming smile. 'She used to say that values and life experiences may remain within us, but it's only the books and genes that we pass down to the next generations. One person's poor health can affect generations to come, as more than 40 per cent of disorders and diseases are linked to the genes passed down from parents and ancestors. Good health is the most valuable asset one can acquire, and good genes are the most precious heritage we can bestow upon future generations. The practices of good health today will benefit the family tomorrow. She always believed that happiness is rooted in good health.

'Now, let me explain what 'E' represents.'

'I know that, Baba,' Shatarupa replied with understanding. 'It's Energy. I am a daughter of your friend and a character in her SMILE story,' she continued with tearful eyes. 'I am supposed to carry it forward to a new generation.'

Baba beamed with pride.

- **Manage Your Energy**

  Every principle the book has discussed, whether it is physiological or psychological, can also be seen as how efficiently we can manage our body's energy. The point to note here is that healthy living is not just about consuming the right energy but also our approach to how we use energy in the most optimal manner. Hence, it is very important for every person to understand how to use energy smartly which, in turn, can help us live a healthy life. On the other hand, if we are not properly managing our energy levels, we are losing out not just on healthy living but also on a happier and successful life. Let's understand it better and see how we can adopt this approach in our life.

Every thought, emotion, and action can be seen as units of energy, and all the body's processes, both conscious and metabolic, require energy. From the moment we contemplate eating a meal to the complex processes of digestion and nutrient absorption, our body expends energy. The gut plays a pivotal role in generating and storing this energy from the food we consume, along with water, sunlight, and air, while the brain manages its distribution.

The interplay between the brain and the gut becomes apparent in times of stress, where the brain redirects more energy to address the crisis, often leading to a loss of appetite. This perspective on energy helps us understand why conditions like depression, illness, or overexertion of muscles demand more energy than usual. Infections, for instance, can significantly deplete energy reserves, leaving us feeling weak and achy during illnesses such as fever.

It's crucial to comprehend how the body allocates and utilises its energy, considering the specific needs of each component. The brain alone consumes 20-25 per cent of the body's total energy, digestion accounts for 10-15 per cent, metabolic activities demand 30 per cent, and physical activities vary but make up the remaining 30-40 per cent. Any imbalance in this energy distribution can lead to compromises in other areas. For instance, when the mind is highly focused or creative, or when the body is burdened with unhealthy foods, it demands more energy, affecting concentration, positivity, and overall vitality.

Effective energy management is an art that the body must practice daily, based on anticipated activities. In sports, for instance, successful coordination between the mind and body before executing a play is paramount. External distractions, like worrying about game outcomes or competitors' performance, can disrupt this coordination. Athletes who excel and become champions are those who master effective energy management. Ultimately, an energy-efficient body and mind are foundational to optimal health.

The story of SMILE has been passed down from one life to another since the beginning of our existence on this planet. It all begins with sharing and passing on the wisdom of good health—from you to your family, our society, our city, our nation, and our world. As this knowledge spreads, our planet becomes a happier and healthier place and you can start by sharing this book. Wishing you good health and a happy life, ever after.

God bless and keep SMILEing.

Final Thoughts

Congratulations on reaching the end of the book and completing your health journey. Hopefully, along the way, you have acquired valuable and practical health secrets and evergreen principles that will empower you to lead a vibrant, fulfilling life filled with well-being and vitality for years to come.

We have explored a comprehensive approach to health that covers daily monitoring, taking charge of your well-being, and gaining a deep understanding of true well-being. This holistic perspective is rarely found in a single health book, making your journey unique and enlightening. But let's not allow these principles to gather dust on the bookshelf. Remember, awareness alone is not enough; true fulfilment comes from putting these principles into action. It's time to make practising good health a daily ritual. As you embrace these principles wholeheartedly, they will become an unstoppable force propelling you towards boundless vitality.

Consider the significance of emotions, the deliberate pursuit of discomfort, and the awareness of the acidic-alkaline balance as potential game-changers in your life from now on. You can begin with the prime FIT principle: be mindful of your emotions at every moment, develop the habit of mapping your emotions using the Mind Compass, purposefully seek out discomfort, demonstrate agility and an active lifestyle, and maintain a balanced acidic-alkaline state. Review and refresh your understanding of the other principles, make a list, and gradually incorporate them into your daily routine. Start with one or two practices, giving yourself ample time to fully integrate them before moving on to others. Over time, many of these principles will evolve to become uniquely yours, shaping your personal definition of health. You will find yourself straddling the line that separates healthy from unhealthy living, and with each conquered principle, you will emerge as a living testament to the power of *Healthy, Ever After.*

Another point to be aware of is that good health is contagious. Share it with those around you. Spread happiness by gifting or recommending this book. By disseminating the principles of healthy living, you contribute to the betterment of society, making these principles accessible and understandable to all. Encourage others to adopt healthier habits, knowing that even one person's positive change can set in motion a chain reaction of healthy living that benefits generations to come.

Preach these health principles and spread happiness. The very purpose of writing this book was to simplify health concepts for everyone to grasp easily. Even if you inspire change in just one person, it marks the beginning of a legacy of healthy living that will echo through generations.

Let this moment be your turning point. Take

ownership of your health and embark on a journey towards a stronger, happier, and more energetic you. No more half-hearted attempts, and no more settling for unhealthy practices. You hold the roadmap to becoming the healthiest version of yourself, and there is no better time to start than now! And trust me, once you have tasted the euphoria of true well-being, there is no better feeling than experiencing good health.

So, get ready to embrace this never-ending journey of life and health. Step into the spotlight of extraordinary healthy living and proudly declare, 'I choose to live healthy, ever after, and experience life happily, ever after!

* * *

'The goal of life is to make your heartbeat match the beat of the universe, to match your nature with nature.'

—Joseph Campbell

Acknowledgements

To begin, I want to express my heartfelt gratitude to you, dear reader. Your trust, interest, and time invested in this book are deeply appreciated. My sincere hope is that this book offers you a fresh perspective on everyday health and points the way toward a happier, stronger, and more vibrant version of yourself.

As for the inception of this book, I can't pinpoint the precise moment it entered my mind. What I do know is that it began as a blank canvas, devoid of any concrete idea or plan for structuring the subject matter. I extend my thanks to that initial spark of inspiration and to all the subsequent moments, people, and experiences that knowingly or unknowingly contributed to my quest to complete this book. You have all been educators, inspirations, and sources of reinforcement along this journey.

I firmly believe that even during challenging times, there is always something positive unfolding. In the case of this book, it was the multiple rejections from publishers that played a pivotal role in its improvement. Each rejection served as an opportunity for refinement, resulting in multiple revisions of the manuscript. I offer my sincere thanks to all the publishers and literary agents who took the time to consider and respond to the manuscript, each step of the way enhancing the quality of the content.

A book, in my view, is a delicate balance between sense and sentence. The sentences can be refined as long as there is a clear sense. Crafting a narrative that engages readers seamlessly is a formidable challenge for many authors. During the early stages of this book's development, individuals like Tara Khandelwal, Sudha Pahwa, Anil Gupta, and Monika Chaudhary played instrumental roles. Their reviews and guidance helped infuse valuable and cohesive sense and sentences into the book, and for that, I am truly grateful.

Throughout years of writing, what any author hopes for is to receive a single encouraging comment that keeps them going. Aditya Jarial, my first contact with Hay House, provided that uplifting comment. It is my hope that the journey will continue to accumulate more such likes and comments. Aditya, thank you for shaping the book from start to finish and for effectively balancing feedback between myself, the marketing team, and the editorial team at Hay House. My gratitude extends to the entire team.

I want to thank my mother for her persistent inquiries about my next book, which served as a driving force to keep me going. Her minute-long blessings every time we spoke were a source of motivation. Monika, my wife, thank you for being the first to provide honest feedback and for not complaining when one of our sofa seats inevitably bore the brunt of months of continuous sitting. To my daughters, Saundarya and Angel, I am grateful for understanding and sparing my weekends for writing, when I should have spent that time with you. To my nephew, Ar. Sankalp Chaudhary, thank you for designing the illustrations.

Lastly, it may sound self-indulgent, but I want to express gratitude to myself. All this while, writing on a subject like health, when I am not a doctor and don't even have a science background, there was some amount of faith that kept me going. I firmly believe that you can have a multitude of people join you on a journey, but it's only when you take those first steps that progress is made. Self-belief is the driving force that encourages us to keep moving forward. Just as self-inspiration is the first step to success, it is also the first step to good health. So, always prioritise self-care and self-belief and keep yourself first!

Once again, I extend my heartfelt thanks to all of you for joining me in spreading the principles of good health.